Hands-On Motion Graphics with Adobe After Effects CC

Develop your skills as a visual effects and motion graphics artist

David Dodds

BIRMINGHAM - MUMBAI

Hands-On Motion Graphics with Adobe After Effects CC

Commissioning Editor: Vijin Boricha
Acquisition Editor: Prachi Bisht
Content Development Editor: Shubham Bhattacharya
Technical Editor: Sayali Thanekar
Copy Editor: Safis Editing
Project Coordinator: Nusaiba Ansari
Proofreader: Safis Editing
Indexer: Manju Arasan
Graphics: Jisha Chirayil
Production Coordinator: Aparna Bhagat

First published: April 2019

Production reference: 1240419

Published by Packt Publishing Ltd.
Livery Place
35 Livery Street
Birmingham B3 2PB, UK.

ISBN 978-1-78934-515-5

www.packtpub.com

`mapt.io`

Mapt is an online digital library that gives you full access to over 5,000 books and videos, as well as industry leading tools to help you plan your personal development and advance your career. For more information, please visit our website.

Why subscribe?

- Spend less time learning and more time coding with practical eBooks and Videos from over 4,000 industry professionals
- Learn better with Skill Plans built especially for you
- Get a free eBook or video every month
- Mapt is fully searchable
- Copy and paste, print, and bookmark content

Packt.com

Did you know that Packt offers eBook versions of every book published, with PDF and ePub files available? You can upgrade to the eBook version at `www.Packt.com` and as a print book customer, you are entitled to a discount on the eBook copy. Get in touch with us at `customercare@packtpub.com` for more details.

At `www.Packt.com`, you can also read a collection of free technical articles, sign up for a range of free newsletters, and receive exclusive discounts and offers on Packt books and eBooks.

Contributors

About the author

David Dodds is an artist with a lifelong love of learning and teaching, which led him to a teaching career at UCLA. He stays on the forefront of the motion graphics industry by working with companies and creating motion graphics for the entertainment industry. David teaches, mentors students, and lectures at various events in connection with the exciting motion graphics industry. He currently lives and works in Los Angeles.

I would like to thank my family and friends for their support. Especially my partner, Bradley Hankey, for believing in me and always encouraging me to follow all my many creative passions! I would also like to thank my colleagues at Packt Publishing and my students at UCLA; I learn so much from you all. Thank you for helping me become a better instructor!

About the reviewer

Luis Medrano started his career as a hand-drawn cartoon animator in 1995 in Panama City, Panama, later becoming a 3D and After Effects artist. In 2003, he moved to the United States, where his distinctive cinematic style earned him recognition in the competitive New York City television market as a design director and animator. His vast experience covers marketing, animation, broadcast production, virtual integration, and live television. A self-proclaimed animation scientist, he is currently writing his theories on Motion Orchestration™. Luis is the recipient of two Emmy awards and three Promax awards for his work in animation. He currently works as a CGI artist and consultant in the New York area.

Packt is searching for authors like you

If you're interested in becoming an author for Packt, please visit `authors.packtpub.com` and apply today. We have worked with thousands of developers and tech professionals, just like you, to help them share their insight with the global tech community. You can make a general application, apply for a specific hot topic that we are recruiting an author for, or submit your own idea.

Table of Contents

Preface

Welcome to this introduction to motion graphics with Adobe After Effects, your guide to motion graphics, the most exciting field in the world today. This book will provide readers with the knowledge and skills required to communicate effectively with After Effects and with the ability to create infographics through the use of feature film-level compositing tools. Other topics covered include editing, camera work, and lighting. You will learn how to create stunning visual effects and exciting animated 3D typography. This book will train readers in the concepts of motion design, examining a range of diverse issues, such as merging graphic design and animation with cinematic storytelling techniques.

Who this book is for

This book is targeted at students, professionals, YouTubers, and people who are interested in video editing, animation, and motion graphics. It is also designed for illustrators who would like to set their creations in motion. All these groups will really enjoy reading this book.

What this book covers

Chapter 1, Getting Started with After Effects, explains where the main tools and menus are to be found. The focus will be on shape and text layers, animating position, scale, rotation, opacity, and masks.

Chapter 2, Creating a Lower Third for a Television Show, talks about precomps. This is a very important part of After Effects. It helps you to create complex animations quickly. Once you understand this concept, we will create a lower third project with more complex layers.

Chapter 3, Using Shape Layers to Create an Animated Lyric Video, builds on the previous chapter in understanding more complex layers. We will also begin working with text animators. Text animators are more complex text tools that allow you to achieve detailed animation using text presets.

Chapter 4, Creating an Infographic with Character Animator, takes your text animation to a more advanced level and uses it to communicate. You will animate icons dynamically. Having an understanding of the graph editor will make your animations more realistic and professional. You will also learn about different tools for animating simple characters to use in your projects.

Chapter 5, Producing a Film Title Project Using Text Animator, explains how opening film titles are a great way to set a mood and communicate what the movie is about (according to Saul Bass, a graphic designer who pioneered motion graphics and contemporary film titles). In this chapter, we are going to create a dynamic film title opening sequence.

Chapter 6, Animating Sports Graphics with Compositing Effects, begins our work with video footage. Understanding how to edit video and add effects to footage is an important tool in After Effects. You will learn how to use tools commonly used in the entertainment industry to composite and track video.

Chapter 7, Developing a VFX Project Using the 3D Camera Tracker, gets more advanced with professional-level visual effects commonly used in the entertainment industry. Understanding how to separate objects from their background opens up a plethora of possibilities in special effects. We will also learn how to use the particle system.

Chapter 8, Creating a 2.5D Environment Camera Fly Through, takes your layers and puts them in the 3D space. After Effects has a powerful 3D workspace. Understanding how to animate in a 3D space opens up a lot of options in terms of creating dynamic videos. In this chapter, you will get up and running with all the 3D tools.

Chapter 9, Building a 3D C4D Lite Logo Project, teaches you how to model, light, and composite your 3D project in After Effects.

To get the most out of this book

Before beginning to use this book, you should have a working knowledge of your computer. You should know how to use the mouse and how to open, save, and close files.

After Effects CC is not included with this book. You need to purchase and install it. Some of the lessons in this book use Adobe Bridge, Photoshop, Illustrator, and Character Animator. You must install these programs from Adobe Creative Cloud.

To work through the projects in this book, you need to download the lesson files. The link is provided in the Technical requirements section of *Chapter 2, Creating a Lower Third for a Television Show.*

Download the color images

We also provide a PDF file that has color images of the screenshots/diagrams used in this book. You can download it here: `https://www.packtpub.com/sites/default/files/downloads/9781789345155_ColorImages.pdf`.

Conventions used

There are a number of text conventions used throughout this book.

`CodeInText`: Indicates code words in text, database table names, folder names, filenames, file extensions, pathnames, dummy URLs, user input, and Twitter handles. Here is an example: "Create a new 1920 x 1080 comp with a frame rate of `29.97`."

Bold: Indicates a new term, an important word, or words that you see on screen. For example, words in menus or dialog boxes appear in the text like this. Here is an example: "Go to **Layer** | **New** | **Solid**, and change the color to blue."

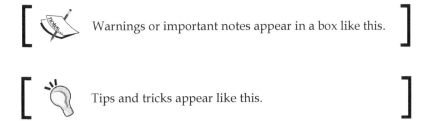

Warnings or important notes appear in a box like this.

Tips and tricks appear like this.

Get in touch

Feedback from our readers is always welcome.

General feedback: If you have questions about any aspect of this book, mention the book title in the subject of your message and email us at `customercare@packtpub.com`.

Errata: Although we have taken every care to ensure the accuracy of our content, mistakes do happen. If you have found a mistake in this book, we would be grateful if you would report this to us. Please visit `www.packt.com/submit-errata`, selecting your book, clicking on the Errata Submission Form link, and entering the details.

Piracy: If you come across any illegal copies of our works in any form on the internet, we would be grateful if you would provide us with the location address or website name. Please contact us at copyright@packt.com with a link to the material.

If you are interested in becoming an author: If there is a topic that you have expertise in, and you are interested in either writing or contributing to a book, please visit authors.packtpub.com.

Reviews

Please leave a review. Once you have read and used this book, why not leave a review on the site that you purchased it from? Potential readers can then see and use your unbiased opinion to make purchase decisions, we at Packt can understand what you think about our products, and our authors can see your feedback on their book. Thank you!

For more information about Packt, please visit packt.com.

Section 1: Text, Layers, Characters, Animation

In this section, you will learn where the main tools and menus are. The focus is on shape and text layers, animating position, scale, rotation, opacity, and masks.

The following chapters are included in this section:

- *Chapter 1, Getting Started with After Effects*

- *Chapter 2, Creating a Lower Third for a Television Show*

- *Chapter 3, Using Shape Layers to Create an Animated Lyric Video*

- *Chapter 4, Creating an Infographic with Character Animation*

- *Chapter 5, Producing a Film Title Project Using Text Animator*

1
Getting Started with After Effects

Welcome to this exciting journey into **After Effects**! In this chapter, I will give you a grand tour of this powerful program.

You will learn to navigate using After Effects and to locate your tools and effects. You will be introduced to the layer panel, the timeline, and key frames, and you will learn to import files. You will also learn to create, animate, and mask your layers.

We'll begin the chapter with the program's interface, to help you understand how to navigate. By the end of this chapter, you will know how to create a simple animated slideshow. The concepts we'll learn in this chapter are simple; however, the tools that we'll learn to use will be crucial to future projects (Illustration, photography, and all artistic content by David Dodds).

This chapter will cover the following topics:

- The After Effects interface
- Masking layers
- Creating a project
- Introducing layer properties
- Basic animation
- Creating an animation slideshow

Technical requirements

To use this book, you will need Photoshop, Illustrator, Character Animator, and After Effects CC. You need to have a good understanding of standard menus and commands. Some of the lessons in this book use Adobe-Character Animator, Adobe Bridge, Adobe Media Encoder, Adobe Illustrator, and Adobe Photoshop. You must install these applications from Adobe Cloud. Some knowledge of Adobe Photoshop and Illustrator will be helpful for performing the projects in this book.

Computer requirements

After Effects requires a minimum of 8 GB of RAM.

Exploring the interface

Now, let's take a look at the After Effects interface. When you first open After Effects, you will see a **Start** menu. Close this by clicking the red X in the upper right-hand top corner:

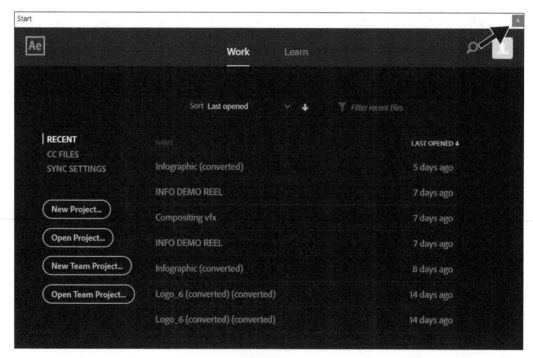

Start menu

This menu can be helpful if you need to locate a recently opened project. I find it best to close this and locate what we need in the program itself.

Resetting the layout

Your workspace is where all your panels and tools are located. This is the heart of the program. Your workspace can be configured in different ways; let's make sure it's set to the default state.

Go to **Window | Workspace | Reset "Standard" to Saved Layout**. This is the standard workspace:

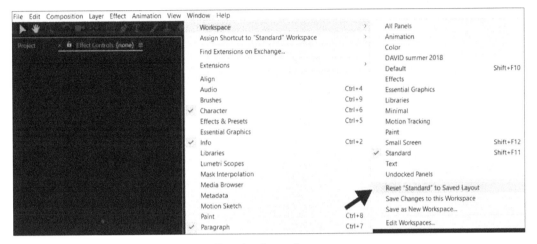

Resetting the workspace

This way, everything is where it's supposed to be in our interface; nothing is out of place.

Saving your project

Saving a project is always a good practice. Let's start our project by creating a new file by saving it:

1. Go up to the top-left tab, **File**. Choose **Save As | Save As...** and name the file `test`.

2. Navigate to where you want to save your After Effect project. It's a good idea to number your projects. Let's name ours `projects_01`.

We have started saving our first project. It's important to start saving things right away.

The project panel

The **project panel** is where you bring in all your assets. After Effects is often used in post-production. You are usually working from many different asset types. Your project can get very disorganized quickly. This is where you keep all your assets tidy. You will be very happy when your project gets more difficult and you have taken the time to keep things organized. It is easier to find things when you have a tidy project. It also helps you to work faster. The project panel has icons at the bottom of the panel. Choose the one called folder:

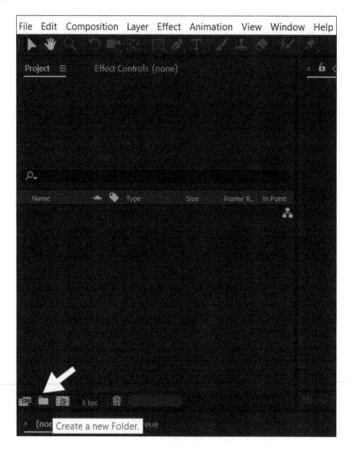

Creating a new folder

Let's learn how to create folders in our project panel by following these steps to create one:

1. Click on the folder icon

2. Name this `new comp-main comp`

When you bring media into After Effects, be sure to organize all your media into the appropriate folders.

You can create the following folders:

- MAIN
- AUDIO
- PRECOMP
- Images
- Footage

You should have five folders. Right-click on the folder to rename them.

The projects in this book will use these five folders. We have created them to organize everything properly.

Importing images

Let's import a large image (at least 1,920 x 1,080) by double-clicking the open area. This brings up your media folders. You can click anywhere in the area where I'm standing in the next screenshot:

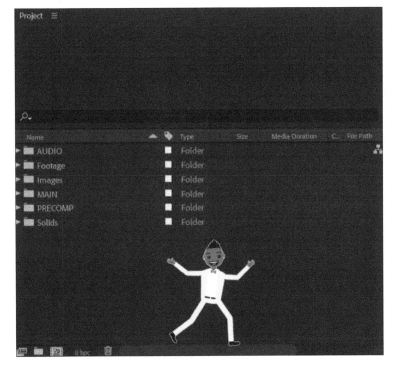

Project panel

Drag and move this image into the Images folder. You can rename your images by right-clicking on the layer.

After Effect references material. It doesn't actually keep anything in the project; it references things. You should never rename a file outside After Effects. When you import images into a Photoshop document, it saves a copy with the document. However, After Effects links to the assets you import into your project. You should always leave the name unchanged because After Effects will not be able to find the new name for its referencing, and you will receive an error message.

Rather than renaming or removing your files from After Effects, it's better to create a copy or not to move it. If you need to replace a file, you have to right-click on the layer and choose to replace or reload the footage:

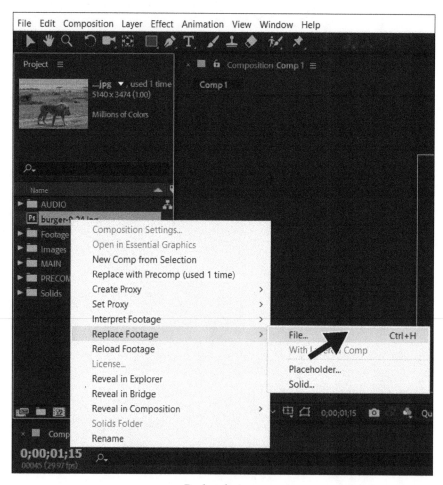

Replace footage

Practice renaming and relinking your files a couple times, just to make sure you understand that concept.

If you need to delete anything, drag it into the trashcan; this is highlighted in the following screenshot:

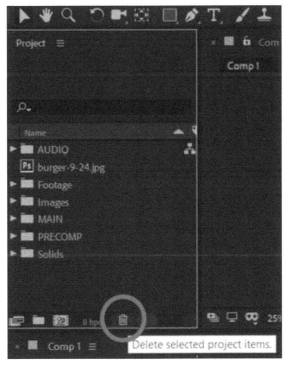

Trashcan

Preferences – Autosave

Now we will turn our attention to setting Auto-Save... for your projects. It's important to get that set up so your project will automatically save, even if you forget to do this. The following steps will show you how to set up autosave:

1. Go to **Edit** | **Preferences** | **Auto-Save...**.
2. Set autosave at 20-minute intervals.

3. You can adjust the maximum number of versions of your project to autosave. The default number is 5:

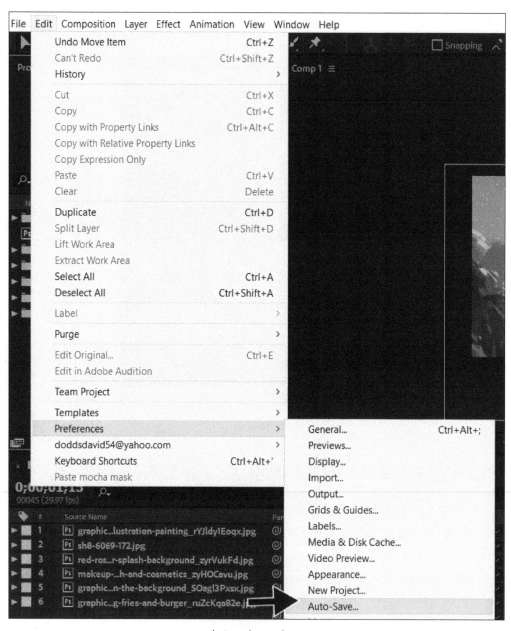

Autosaving projects

Setting up autosave can save your life. If your project crashes, you will be happy that you have a back-up copy saved in the autosave folder. This is located wherever you save your project.

Creating compositions

After Effects uses compositions to place and arrange your elements. Remember to consider design principles that help create a strong composition when you arrange your elements. In After Effects, these compositions are referred to as comps. I am going to create a comp by hitting the new composition icon. If you look closely at the icon, you will see that it looks like a composition symbol with shapes:

New composition

Leave all these settings as they are, but make the comp size 1,920 x 1,080, and make the time duration 0;04;00;00. Name the comp MAIN:

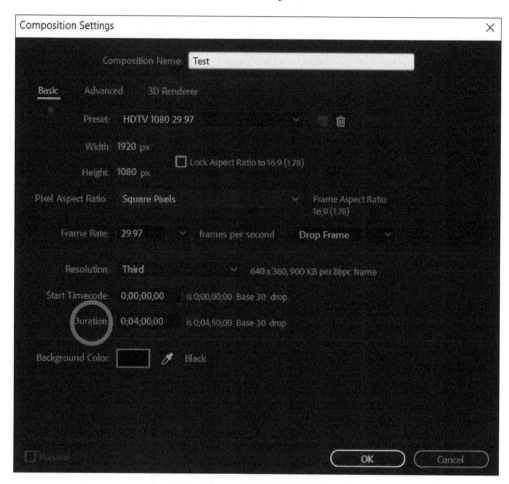

Composition settings

Drag the main comp into the MAIN comp folder:

Organizing a project

The timelines and the toolbar

Look at the lower-third of the screen. This is called the **timeline panel**. The timeline is the works space where you create key frames. This is where you make your layers animate across time. You also organize your layer-stacking order. This stacking order is similar to Photoshop. Layers at the top will appear on top of other layers:

Timeline panel

After briefly learning about the timeline panel, let's discuss how to bring layers into your composition.

Bringing layers into your composition

Bringing layers into your composition is easy. Layers are the basic building blocks for creating a movie. A layer can be an image, video footage, or an audio file.

Follow these steps:

1. Go into the IMAGE folder.

2. Drag the image on to the timeline.

3. If the image is 1,920 x 1,080, it will fit perfectly and fill up the screen. It will come into the comp centered:

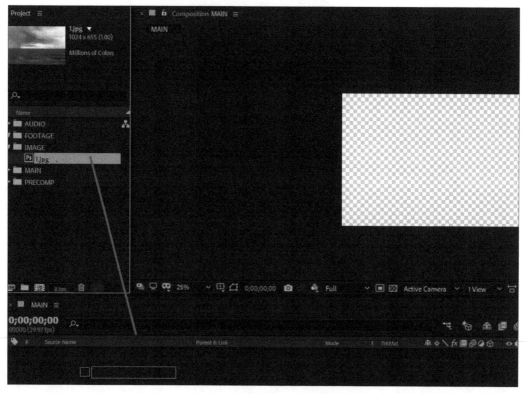

Bringing an image into the timeline

Tool panel

Let's go over our tools! The **tool panel** is where you find all your tools to edit your layers. Here, you can find tools to move your layers and navigate around your composition:

- **Selection Tool (V)**: Go to the top left side of the screen. This is called the **tool bar**:

Selection Tool

  The arrow icon on the far left is called the Selection Tool.

- **Hand Tool (H)**: The hand tool is to the right of the arrow tool. This tool lets you move around in your composition:

Hand Tool

  Now select the hand tool or use the keyboard shortcut H. You can use the hand tool to move around in your view or navigate around in the comp.

- **Zoom Tool (Z)**: The zoom tool is next to the hand tool. This tool will magnify your image in the composition. Select the zoom tool, or use the keyboard shortcut Z, and click on the image in the comp a few times:

Zoom Tool

- **Rotate Tool (W):** The rotate tool is the circular tool next to the zoom tool:

Rotate Tool

Let's explore how to use the rotate tool. The center of the screen where your image is displayed is called the **composition window**. At the bottom left is an icon called the **Magnification ratio popup**. Choose **fit to 100%**. This will zoom out so we can see what's happening:

Magnifying

Select the rotate tool, or use the keyboard shortcut *W*, and adjust the image:

Rotate

To undo an action, go to the top-left corner and choose **Edit | Undo Rotate Object**:

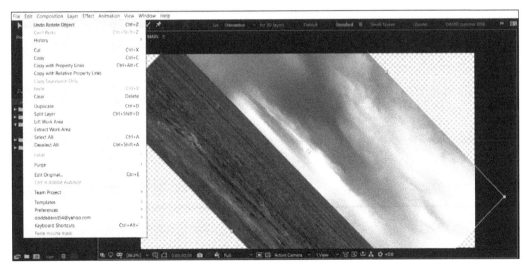

Undo

- **Pan Behind (Anchor Point) Tool (Y)**: I'll skip the camera tool for now. Next to the camera tool is the **pan behind** tool. Use this to move your anchor point. Things animate along the anchor point in After Effects. It's useful to know how to move the anchor point around, as it gives you control over how things animate:

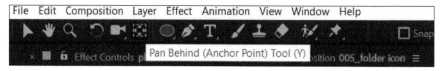

Pan behind tool

- **Masking Tool**: To the right are our masking tools. The first shape in the list is the rectangle tool. With these masking tools, you can click and drag to create a shape. Click on the triangle icon on the bottom-left of this tool's button. You will find the rounded **Rectangle Tool**, the **Eclipse Tool**, and the **Star Tool**:

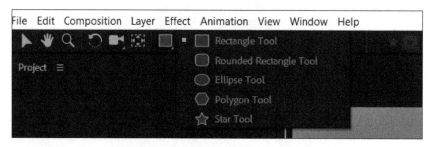

Masking tool

- **Pen Tool (G)**: Next to the rectangle tool is the pen tool. It is used to make custom shapes in After Effects.

- **Type tool**: To the right of the pen tool is the type tool.

- **Brush tool**: The next icon with the brush icon is the brush tool.

- **Stamp tool**: The icon with the stamp icon is the clone stamp tool.

We will go over more of these tools later.

Hopefully, you are starting to get used to the interface in After Effects. Poke around and experiment with these tools, to get comfortable with them. A little triangle next to a tool's button means you can access more options for that tool. If a tool is grayed out, just click on your comp and it will become active.

Preview panel

Let's go over the preview panel. This is located in the upper-right corner of your screen:

Preview panel

This preview panel gives you options such as moving through your movie. A project is made up of frames, just like in real video footage. In After Effects, moving within a project is referred to as *moving down the timeline*. This timeline is represented in units, such as frames, seconds, and minutes. This preview panel allows you to move forward or backward frame by frame. Pressing the **play** button lets you preview your project. You can also use the **ram review**, which gives you the ability to watch the project at a faster speed. You can also hit the space bar to preview your animation.

Composition window

At the bottom of the composition window, there are a few options. Let's go over some of them.

The icon in the lower right-hand corner of the composition is where you will find your guide options. These guide options are used to arrange your layers and to create compositionally strong images. However, these guides are not rendered; they are only for preview purposes:

- **Guides**: These are used for aligning and arranging layers. To remove guides, choose **View | Clear guides**.
- **Title/Action Safe**: These are video-safe zones, for standard video monitors.
- **Rulers**: This is used to drag guides to the composition to align and arrange layers to.
- **Grid**: This is a modular grid that helps you organize your layers and create strong compositions:

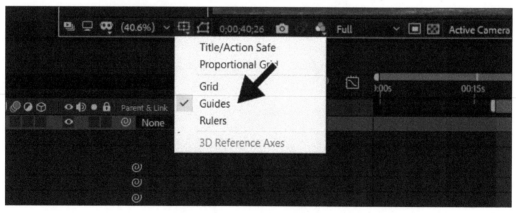

Guides

A little further over to the right is the resolution button. You can reduce the quality down to **Quarter**. This gives you the ability to look at it and play it back even faster, but at a lower quality:

Resolution

Next, we will go over our **Effects & Presets** panel. The effects panel is a major toolbox full of effects to make your video look amazing! This panel gives you access to hundreds of effects that can help you create animation, correct the color, or fix any number of problems with video or images.

Effects panel

The effects panel is located to the far-right, below the preview panel. A lot of these effects are the same as those used in Photoshop. You may be familiar with **Brightness**, **Contrast**, **Curves**, and so on. Make sure your layer is selected in the timeline, before clicking on an effect.

You can add an effect to a layer by doing the following:

1. Twirl the category name dow

2. Click on the effect with the layer selected, or you can type in the name of the effect

3. Double-click on the effect, while your layer is selected

Let's type the effect (auto levels) into the search bar. Double-click the effect to add to our layer:

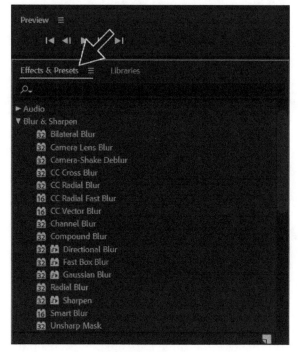

Effects & Presets

You can adjust this effects in the **effects** control panel. This panel is nested right next to your main project panel:

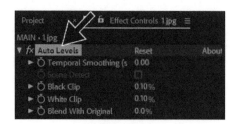

Auto levels

The main difference between these effects and Photoshop is that you can animate them across the timeline, which we will get into in the next sections. You can also add multiple effects to a layer, to create complex visual images.

Introducing layer properties

Duplicating layers is an essential tool that you need to master very quickly. This is helpful because you can reuse layers in your project:

1. Select your layer.
2. You can either hit *Ctrl + D/command + D* on Windows or macOS, respectively, or just choose **Edit | Duplicate** from the menu:

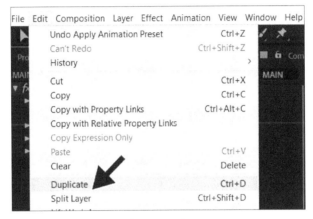

Duplicating an image

When you follow this process, your layer is duplicated. This duplicated layer is an exact copy of the layer. Look closely at your layer and find the triangle to the far right. Click on this triangle. This is called **twirling down**:

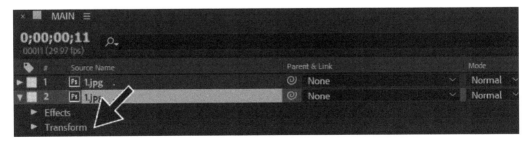

Twirling down properties

Twirling down your layer will reveal the **Transform** properties. Twirl down the triangle icon to the left of the word **Transform**. You will see the **Transform** properties: **Scale**, **Rotation**, **Opacity**, and **Position**. All of these have shortcuts.

Here are the shortcuts for your layer transform properties:

- The shortcut for the scale is S
- The shortcut for rotation is R
- For opacity, the shortcut is T
- For position, the shortcut is.. yep, you guessed it, P

These shortcuts are easy to remember. The only shortcut that's not self-explanatory is T for opacity. An easy way to remember that is to think of T for transparency, or that T is the last syllable of opacity (opaci-T):

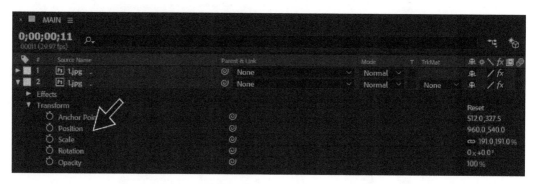

Transform properties

To select anything in After Effects, you need to have the selection tool selected. Navigate to that tool in the upper left-hand corner of your screen in the tool bar. Choose the top layer of the timeline:

Selecting the top layer

With this layer selected, we are going to select our scale property. To use the shortcut, simply hit the letter S. You will see that this reveals the scale property only. Let's adjust the scale parameter. To the far right of the word scale, you will see two numbers. Scrub either one of those parameters to the left. This will shrink this layer down in size:

Scaling down the image

As you can see, this layer scales down in the center of the screen.

Layer panel

Now I will talk to you about our layers and our timeline. It's very important to know your way around this part of the interface. This layer panel is how you control the way your images move. This is where you can see, at a glance, what's going on in your movie. This panel is similar to Photoshop's layer panel. Each one of these icons to the right of the layer has an important function. If you hover your selection arrow over any of these icons, a description will appear on the screen:

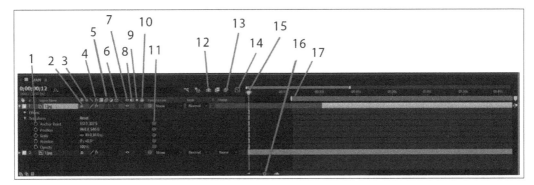

Layer panel

Let's take a closer look some of the buttons and switches of the layer panel:

1. The animation stopwatch
2. The shy button
3. The continuously rasterized button
4. The visual effects button
5. Motion blur
6. The 3D button
7. The hide switch
8. The audio switch
9. The solo button
10. The lock switch
11. The parenting pick whip
12. The shy switch
13. Motion blur
14. Graph editor
15. Current time editor
16. The zoom-in timeline
17. Workspace

Looking at all these buttons and switches can be overwhelming. Let's look at handful of switches that you will find helpful for organizing your layers:

- **#7 The eyeball switch**: This is to the far right of your layer. Turning off the eyeball next to the layer determines whether that layer is seen.

- **#9 The solo switch**: The circle icon to the far right of your layer is called the solo switch. The solo switch will isolate a layer that has that solo turned on.

- **#10 The lock switch**: This is for locking your layers.

- **#12 The shy switch**: If this is turned on in both of these locations, you will not see that layer.

- **#13 The motion blur switch**: This also needs to be activated in both of these locations (#5 and #13); this will enable motion blur.

The footage panel

The **footage panel** is used for previewing your footage. There are also some tools that work only in the footage panel.

To access the footage panel, double-click on the layer. However, this panel is often accessed by accident. It's accessed when double-clicking on a layer. You can tell you're in this panel when you see the white bar at the bottom. There are specific things you can do in this layer, but we usually don't need to be in this panel. Here is a screenshot of the footage panel:

Footage panel

You will find this is a mistake that happens frequently. To get out of this panel, go to the top of that panel and choose the name of your main comp. Or you can reset the workspace area back to the saved layout:

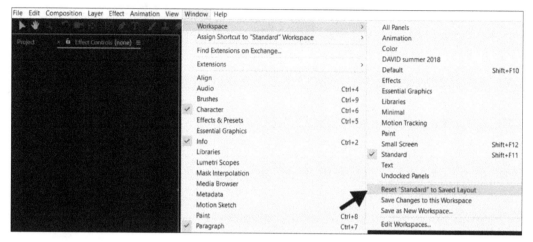

Resetting layout

Resetting this will not change anything in your project. It simply restores your workspace area to the default standard layout.

The timeline panel

Let's talk about time. The **timeline panel** is one of the main things that differentiates After Effects from Photoshop. Unlike Photoshop, After Effects has the ability to make things happen across time. Another big difference between After Effects and Photoshop is 3D space. You can create compositions with 3D depth. After Effect movies are comprised of frames, just like real films.

The timeline lifespan

Think of the timeline like a lifespan. The beginning is the timeline's birth and at the end of your work area, that's considered the death or the end of the lifespan.

Zooming into the timeline

You can zoom into any point of the timeline with the button at the lower-center of the timeline. Or you can zoom into your timeline by moving the slider. If you look closely, you can you can see (F), which stands for **frames**:

Zooming into the slider

The timeline is measured with time codes. The F next to the numbers on the timeline stands for frames.

Navigating in the timeline

The timeline is always moving from left to right:

- Use the *Page Up* key as a shortcut to navigate forward in the timeline, frame by frame, and *Page Down* to navigate backward in the timeline, frame by frame.

- A shortcut for moving down one frame in the timeline is *Page Down* or *Ctrl* + the right arrow (on a PC) or *Page Down* or *command* + the right arrow (on macOS). You can also use the arrows in the preview panel:

Preview panel

The f on the timeline stands for frames; the numbers represent the number of frames:

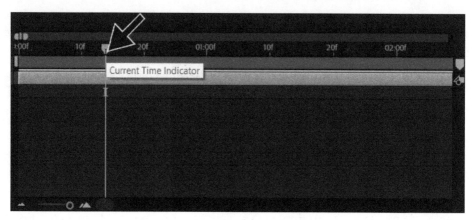

Frames

Go to the beginning of the timeline. The shortcut is for this is pressing the home button on the numeric keypad.

Current time indicator

This guitar pick-shaped object highlighted in the following screenshot is called the **current time indicator icon**. Moving this time indicator is another way to navigate through the timeline:

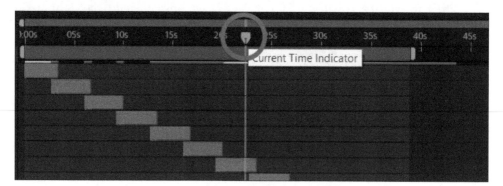

Current time indicator

The workspace area

The timeline is the entire length of your composition. Your **workspace area** is the length of your movie. This is also called the **rendering area**. When I hit the play button for previewing my movie, it happens within that space. This can be trimmed and edited. To trim your workspace area, perform the following steps:

1. Move your time indicator to the desired spot on the timeline
2. Press the letter N to activate the shortcut to trim the work area

There is usually more than one way to do something in After Effects. To manually trim your workspace, perform the following steps:

1. Move your mouse to the beginning the timeline and hover over the blue bar. This is the start of your workspace area.
2. Drag this bar to the right, to trim your work area.

You can drag either the start or the end or the workspace area. Trimming this shortens the duration of the comp. This is useful for previewing your movie or previewing a small section of your movie. Remember when you export or render your movie, this workspace needs to be trimmed, to reflect exactly what you want exported. The duration of the workspace is the only thing that will be exported or rendered:

Trimming the workspace area

Trimming layers

You can edit the duration of your layers by trimming them. Trimming your layers will give you control when your layers appear in your movie:

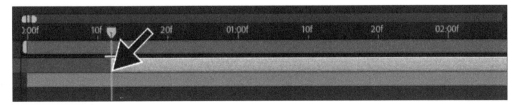

Trimming layers

To trim your layer, perform the following steps:

1. Move your time indicator to the desired spot on the timeline

2. Press *Alt + [* or *Option + [* on macOS to activate the shortcut to trim your layer

To manually trim your layer, perform the following steps:

1. Move your time indicator to the desired spot on the timeline.

2. Bring your selection tool to the very beginning of the layer and hover over the start of the layer. You will see the trim layer icon represented by two arrows. (You must see this or your dragging you're layers, which is different to trimming them.) Use this to drag and trim your layer.

You can trim any type of layer using the preceding methods. This layer will be trimmed exactly where the time indicator is. Move your time indicator back and forth in the timeline across this trimmed layer. See how the layer appears where the image is trimmed to? This is how layers can appear across time.

Creating composition markers on your timeline

You can further organize your timeline by adding information to the timeline. You can also create markers, notes, and metadata on your timeline. These markers can also be used to align layers to a point in the timeline. The following are the steps for creating a composition marker:

1. Hit *Shift* and a number.

2. Double-click that number to enter a note:

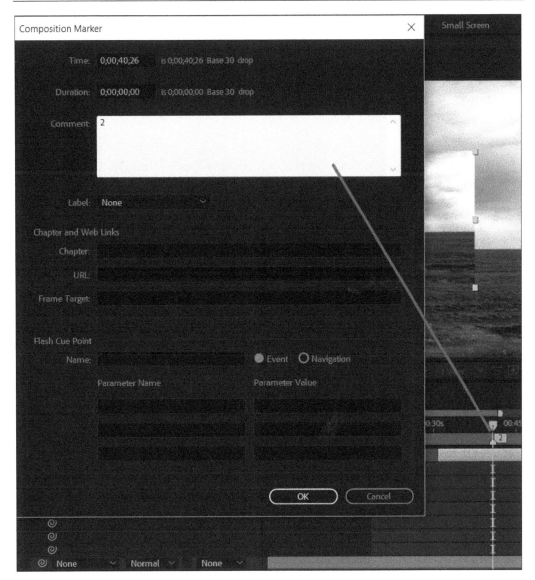

Composition markers

These markers and notes can be particularly helpful when organizing your project and writing notes from clients and team members.

Animating a property

Animating a property is essentially marking a parameter in time and adjusting that property further down the timeline. We create animation by creating at least two key frames. The steps to animate a property are simple. But you need to be sure you follow these steps each time. When you want to animate any property, you need to perform the following steps:

1. First hit the stopwatch, which will automatically create a key frame for you.

2. Move down the timeline, and change the **Transform** property to whatever you want it to be. That will automatically create a blue diamond key frame for you. But you have to be sure and press the stopwatch first.

After you have created key frames, you're free to move and adjust those key frames. Later, I will get into a lot more detail regarding adjusting key frames.

Animating scale

You can animate your scale parameter to make your layer change in scale over time. Follow these steps to begin your animation journey:

1. Press the keyboard shortcut *S* for the scale parameter to come up.

2. Indicate in the timeline where you want the animation to begin.

3. Hit the stopwatch for scale.

4. Page down to the right, getting closer to the end of this animation.

5. Scrub the scale parameter. This will automatically create a blue diamond key frame.

Let's preview that. If I want to give my layer a little bit of blur, I'll hit the blur icon. Look in the timeline:

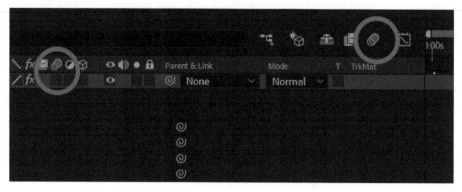

Motion blur

This is an effect that has to be turned on in two places. It has to be turned on in the timeline, just above the timeline. If you hit the preview button, you will see how it gives it a nice blur. That's how things move in real life. There is always some sort of blur when things move fast.

Solid layers and masking

Solid layers are basic colored layers. These can be used to give your video a solid color in the background. We can also use solid layers to create more complex masks. Let's spend more time with basic solid layers. Solid layers are simple color layers that can be edited with masking tools. You will learn how to create solids, edit them, and mask them:

1. Create a new comp.
2. Make the composition dimensions 1,920 x 1,080.
3. Name this comp `solids test`.
4. Move this composition into the main `comp` folder.
5. Create a basic solid layer, **Layer | New | Solid**, or you can hit the shortcut *Ctrl + Y* or *command + Y* on macOS.
6. Click on the color box and change the color to yellow:

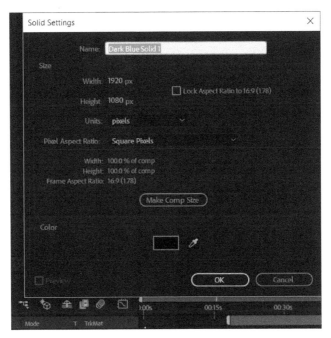

Solid settings

Good job! You have created your first solid layer. Notice that when you create a solid layer, After Effects creates a folder named solids in your project window. Whenever you create a new solid, it will automatically go into that folder. Right now, you have only one layer in your comp. It gets complicated when there are many layers in your composition. Let's create more layers to get used to working with more than one layer:

1. Create another solid, or use a shortcut *Ctrl + Y* or *command+ Y* for macOS.
2. Make this solid orange.
3. Move this new orange layer to the lower-right corner.
4. Create another solid, or use the shortcut *Ctrl + Y* or *command + Y* for macOS.
5. Make this solid blue. Move this layer to the upper-left corner.

Remember that the stacking order is really important in After Effects. You will see what is on top first, followed by what is on the bottom, which is on the background. This composition is created with layers stacked on top of one another. You can see what's underneath that layer. You can see there are other things in the background. There is a solid underneath that layer. At this point, you should see all your different-colored layers: some in front of the others, and some at the back. This is a good visual representation of the stacking order. Look in the timeline; you can see how the stacking order correlates to what you see in your composition:

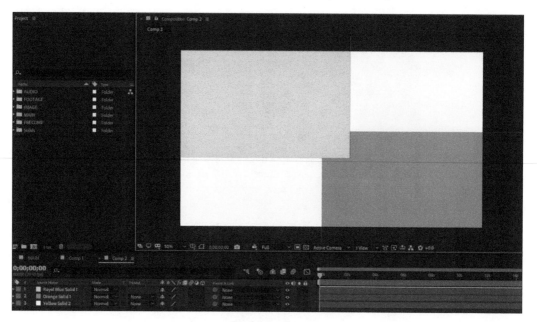

Stacking order

Let's look at the transparency parameters for our solid layers. You can access this by pressing the letter *T*. Scrub this parameter to reduce the opacity, and then lower the opacity. Notice you can still see the other layers through it:

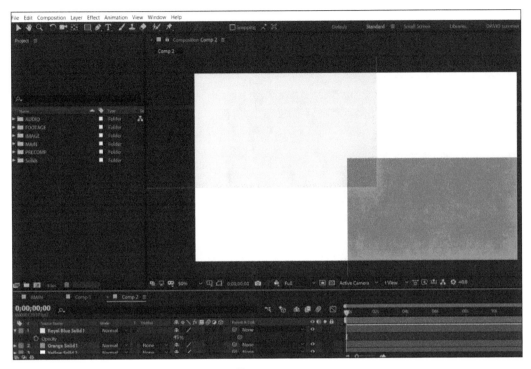

Transparancy

Now that you have learned how to change your layer opacity, let's learn how to duplicate layers.

Duplicating layers

In After Effects, duplicating your layers will create an exact copy of your layers and any key frames and effects you have on them. To duplicate your layer, perform the following steps:

1. First, select the layer, duplicating your latest layer
2. Press *Ctrl* + *D*, or *command* + *D* for macOS

3. To change the setting for your solid layer, press *Shift + Ctrl + Y* or *Shift + command + Y* for macOS

 Your shortcut may be different if you have macOS. Refer to tab at the right of the After Effects panels, | **Help** | **Keyboard Shortcuts...**:

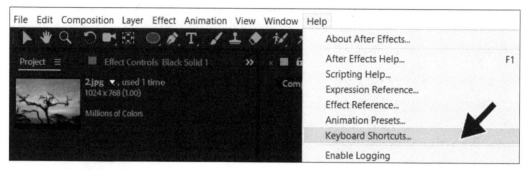

Keyboard shortcuts

If you find anything you're doing a lot, find the shortcut for it. Learning these shortcuts will greatly speed up your workflow in After Effects.

Identifying and turning off your layers

When you get more advanced with After Effects, you will have many layers in your timeline. One way to identify a layer is to turn off all the other layers. Another reason to temporarily turn off a layer is to see how your composition looks without that layer. These eyeball icons are for turning off your layers:

Eyeball icon

Remember when the eyeball is visible, it means that the layer is visible. When it's not visible, the layer will not be seen in the composition.

Solo layers

Soloing your layer can be a life-saver. This will help you temporarily show one single layer or many single layers at a time. What makes this switch so important is that it's easy to turn on and off without changing any of your original layers. It's also easy to tell which layers you have soloed, making it easy to turn off the solo switch when you need to. To activate the solo switch, simply turn on the solo button. If you solo something, you will see the grid behind it, and this grid means that it is a transparent background. Turn off the solo switch to return the layer to its original condition. This becomes really helpful when you have a lot of layers and you want to locate and identify and work with just one layer; you can solo it:

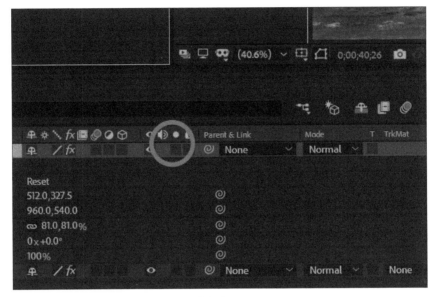

Solo layer

Understanding how to solo your layers will help you quickly turn on and off hundreds of layers with no fear of ruining anything. Try practicing with the solo button on a layer.

Tagging your layers

Tagging your layers can be especially helpful for identifying and organizing your layers in the timeline. You can change these tags to be any color you want. When you need to quickly edit something, sometimes you can select it, but sometimes it can be really hard to find it. Identifying layers is an important part of After Effects. When you have a very complicated project, it's very important to be able to identify your layers. This is when naming and tagging your layers correctly becomes very important. Organization is very important:

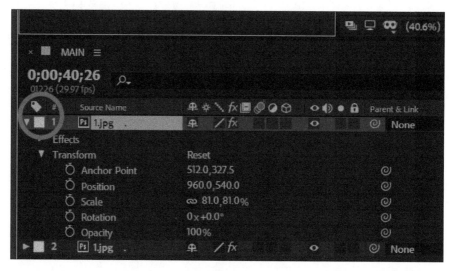

Tags

In After Effects, your composition window is like a stage. You can see images outside the frame or stage. You can also drag things into or out of the main stage area. This is helpful when you want to start your animation off-screen and end up on-screen.

Looking at transform properties

Your layers have **transform properties**, which are the heart and soul of animation. Anything that has a stopwatch next to it can be animated. All these parameters can be overwhelming at first glance. Let's go over each property shortcut to familiarize yourself with them all. Twirl word transform down to see all the properties:

- **Anchor Point**: The shortcut is Y
- **Position**: The shortcut is P
- **Scale**: The shortcut is S

- **Rotation**: The shortcut is R

- **Opacity**: The shortcut is T

- **Reveal all key frames**: The shortcut is U

Pressing any of these keyboard shortcuts while your layer is selected will bring up that parameter:

Transform properties

All these transform properties can be animated across time. All such properties appear with the icon of a stopwatch, which indicates the feature of animating them in the timeline.

Rulers and guides

After Effects comes with different guides you can use to create more precise alignments of your objects. If you look at the top-right of your tool panel, you can enable **Snapping**:

Snapping

This will make your objects snap to your guides. In the **Guides** section, you will find a variety of guides and grids to go beyond the guesswork of lining up your object in After Effects. The guide **Title/Action Safe** is used for video monitors. These guides can be accessed at the bottom of the composition window by clicking the grid icon:

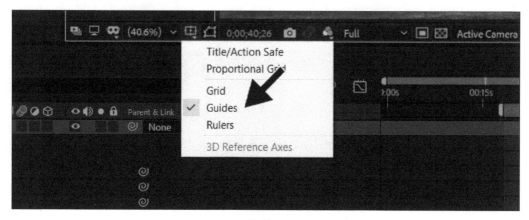

Guides

If you choose the **Rulers** option, you have access to guides that you can drag across your composition and align objects to the guides:

Custom guides

Guides can be a great help to layout your composition and arrange text precisely.

Editing masks

In this section, we are going to discuss masking and editing layers and solids. We are going to mask off or cut out parts of the solids to create a shape. The following steps will illustrate how to do it:

1. Create a 1,920 x 1,080 comp.

2. Create a new solid layer layer, | **New solid**, or **Ctrl + Y** or **command + Y** for macOS.

3. Make the solid yellow.

Look at the top-right of your tool bar. Under the **Rectangle Tool**, you have a variety of masking shapes to edit your solid. These are the masking tools that shape with After Effects. You can choose a **Rectangle Tool**, a **Rounded Rectangle Tool**, an **Ellipse Tool**, a **Polygon Tool**, or a **Star Tool**:

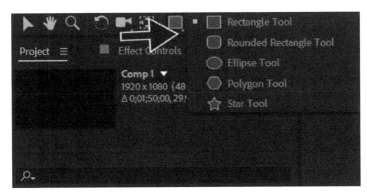

Mask tools

We are going to practice using an ellipse tool to cut out our shape:

1. Choose **Ellipse Tool**

2. Choose where you want to create your shape

3. Click and drag

When dragging these tools, the mask may stretch. If you don't want that, hit *Shift* while dragging. That will create a perfect shape.

Editing your mask shape

Click once on one of the squares in the bounding box, and insert an image of the masking solid:

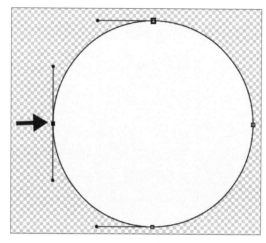

Selecting a single point

The square will fill and you will get bezier handles. This enables you to edit one single mask point:

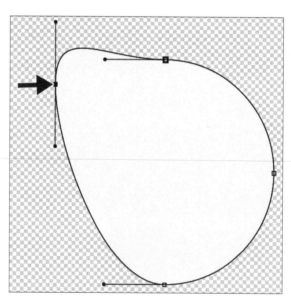

Editing a single point

To edit the entire mask:

1. Double-click one of these squares.

2. You will get a square bounding box.

3. Drag this bounding box to edit all the points at the same time:

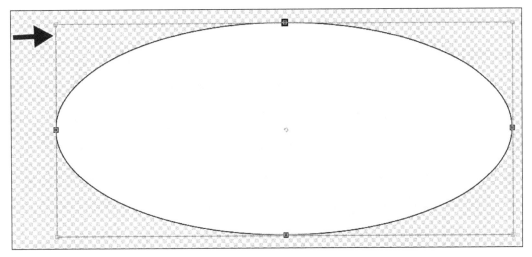

Masking a bounding box

This is masking off the rest of the solid. Under the properties for masking, there is a mask column where you can choose other parameters. This will hide your mask or give you different masking options.

Editing masks

You can take these basic shapes and make other more complex shapes. You can also change the color of the mask by clicking on the color box in the mask. After Effects also has other parameters that you can work with. Clicking on the mask gives you other parameters that can be edited. You can edit this mask by adjusting the feathering parameter. Adjusting the feathering amount means the outside of the mask will be feathered. Of course, the feathering is able to be key-framed. You can expand the mask as well. The expansion can also go the opposite direction, so you'll actually be eating into the mask in the negative direction. I'd like for you to experiment with all these mask-editing parameters.

Using the subtract-masking feature

Masking is a very powerful tool used for roto scoping and creating shapes. You have control over how your mask will behave, and you can choose to add or subtract from your mask shape. We will focus on the subtract feature:

1. Drag another shape on top of the current solid shape.

2. Find the new mask parameter on that solid in the lower-left side of the timeline.

3. To the right of the mask is a tab called **Add** with an arrow pointing down. Click on that.

4. Choose **Subtract** from that list:

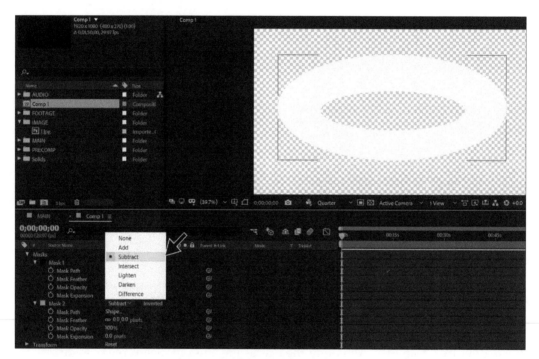

Subtract mask

See how it cuts that shape out? This is how you can create interesting shapes in After Effects. Have a lot of fun with this; there's so much you can do with it—the sky's the limit! Masking becomes very important when you need to cut layers, videos, images, and so on. Think of layers as scissors to cut out what you don't want to see. I'd like for you guys to play with these shapes. Start editing these mask points. You can create complex interesting shapes with these techniques.

Creating an animated slideshow

After all the knowledge we have acquired so far, it is imperative that we put it to use. Let's make a simple animated slideshow, using the tips and tricks we have learned so far in this chapter. Follow these steps:

1. Create a 1,920 x 1,080 comp and call it `slideshow`. Make the comp 20 seconds long.

2. Move into the main `comp` folder.

3. Import four photos (each with 1,920 x 1,080 dimensions).

4. Put the photos into the `image` folder.

5. Make a new solid: **Layer | New solid**. Call this back, and make the color black.

6. Bring your first image into the timeline.

7. Hit S to get your scale. Adjust this so your image fits in the frame.

8. Spend some time adjusting your image in the comp. You may not need to adjust the scale. However, if you need to adjust the size of your image, press S to get the scale parameter.

9. Scrub the scale parameter to get the desired size:

Scaling an image

Let's add additional images to our slide show project. Follow these steps for adding images to your composition:

1. Bring in a second image
2. Adjust the scale
3. Repeat these steps for the remaining images
4. Select these layers and trim them so they are 3 seconds long

We are going trim our layers in the timeline. This will ensure that each image will be seen in the slide show for a certain amount of time:

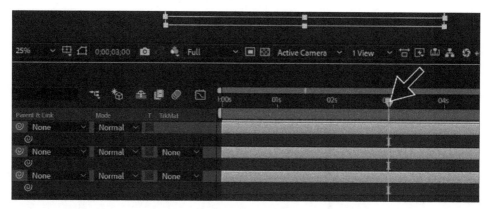

Trimming layers

Let's follow these steps to trim the layers:

1. Select all layers to go to 3 second in the timeline
2. Select *Alt + R* bracket/*option + R* bracket (macOS) to trim the layers, or you can drag the layers to trim them

It's important to understand how to trim your layers for this project and other projects we will work on. Make sure your layers are lined up and trimmed:

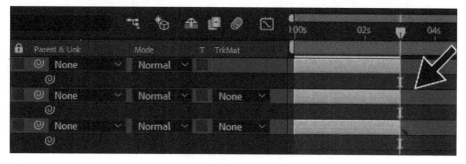

Lining up the layers

After Effects has different types of assistance to help you with animation functions. We are going to use sequence layers. This will sort our layers across time. You can find this animation assistance on the top animation tab of your project window:

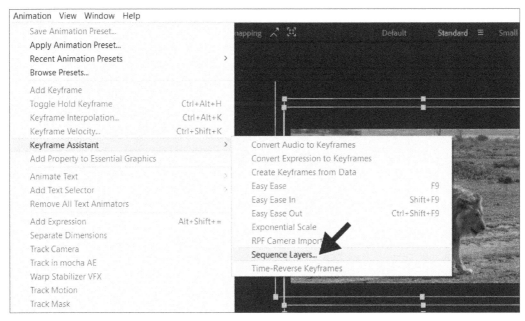

Sequence layers

Select **All layers | Animation | Keyframe Assistance | Sequence Layers....**

Notice that After Effects takes your layers and sequences them across your timeline evenly! The next step for our slideshow is at the end:

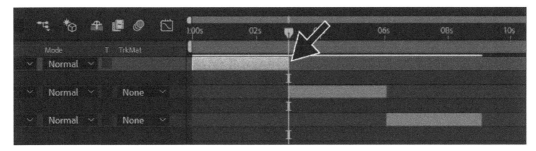

End of layer

The next step is to go 20 frames from the end of your layers (count backward from the end of the layer):

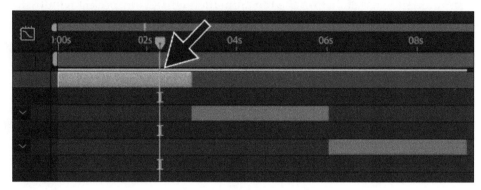

20 key frames

Next we are going to create a fadeout animation for our images:

1. Press *T* for the opacity parameter.

2. Click on the stop watch for opacity. This creates a key frame, which is the first step of any animation.

3. Go forward 20 key frames. Turn the opacity down to 0.

Your timeline should have two key frames. The first key frame is 100% opacity, and the last one will be 0% opacity.

You can test the animation by dragging the time indicator over the key frames. The image should be fading out:

Opacity

To make the layer beneath this image fade on as the top image is fading off, we need to adjust this second image:

1. Select the layer beneath the top layer.

2. Drag your bottom layer, or choose *Alt + L* bracket to trim your layer to that point.

The top layer will begin to fade out as the layer shown next will appear or fade on:

Adjusting the second layer

The goal is to have each photo fade into the next layer. This will happen over the course of 20 frames. It will be a slow fade. Repeat the preceding steps for each layer, and then proceed as follows:

1. Add a black solid layer, for the background

2. Move this layer to the bottom of the layers

   One of the most common things that new After Effects users forget to do is trim the work area at the end of a project:

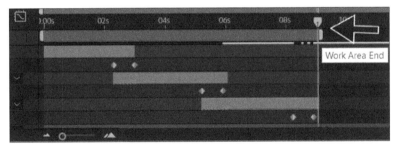

Slideshow trim work area

3. Drag the blue bar over from the right.

4. Drag this to the end of your layers, or move your time indicator at the end of your last layer and press the keyboard shortcut N, to trim the work area.

The final step is to preview your slideshow. Look for anything you'd like to adjust. You can always tweak any of the settings after creating a project.

Congratulations! You've created your first animated project in this book!

Press the space bar to preview your animated slideshow!

Summary

I hope you enjoyed your grand tour of After Effects. We learned about the interface and how to import, edit, and mask layers. Most importantly, we learned how to animate! The basics of animation is key as you work on projects. Grasping these fundamentals will propel you forward to understanding even more complex tools and concepts. Learning the interface and the basic animation are basic but important blocks for building your amazing future with motion graphics!

In *Chapter 2, Creating a Lower Third for a Television Show*, we will animate using the **Easy Ease** assistant. We will also work with null objects to animate a lower-third project. We will use masking and animation tools introduced in this chapter. You will also learn how to create type and how to use **precomps**.

Questions

1. What are the steps for creating an animation?
2. How do you trim or extend a layer in the timeline?
3. How do you trim or extend the workspace area?
4. Where are the safe guides located?
5. How do you advance one key frame down the timeline?
6. How do you preview your movie?
7. How do you create a solid layer?
8. Where are your masking shapes located?
9. How do you edit one single masking point?
10. How do you edit all the masking points at once?
11. How do you apply the subtract masking?
12. What is a key frame?
13. How are key frames represented on the timeline?
14. How are seconds represented on the timeline?

Further reading

- To understand more about guides and using views, check out the following: `https://helpx.adobe.com/after-effects/using/modifying-using-views.html`

- To understand more about the timeline in After Effects, click on this link: `https://helpx.adobe.com/after-effects/using/composition-basics.html#timeline_panel`

- More information about masking tools can be found here: `https://helpx.adobe.com/after-effects/using/creating-shapes-masks.html#create_a_shape_or_mask_by_dragging_with_shape_tools`

- To understand more about key frames and animation, follow this link: `https://helpx.adobe.com/after-effects/using/setting-selecting-deleting-keyframes.html#Whatarekeyframes`

2
Creating a Lower Third
for a Television Show

In this chapter, we will create a television lower third. Lower thirds are used in television advertising. They provide information about a program. It is useful to know how to create lower thirds because understanding them helps you to understand how to design for television graphics. You will also learn about typography and how to work in the lower third of the screen.

The following topics will be covered in this chapter:

- Designing with storyboards
- Editing masks and using precomps
- Nesting precomps and using the pen tool
- Parenting and null object animations
- Parenting null animations
- Positioning a lower third
- Adjusting colors
- Adjusting masks
- The type tool
- Easy ease
- Rendering options

Technical requirements

You must have Adobe Media Encoder and Adobe Bridge installed on your computer.

The technical requirements for this chapter are the same as *Chapter 1, Getting Started with After Effects*.

Purchase of this book comes with project files for each chapter, so you can learn as you follow along. Follow the links below to download the project files.

Password link:

```
http://www.daviddodds.net/password.html
```

Download link:

```
http://daviddodds.net/login.php?redirect=/after-effects-intro-assets.
html
```

Animating a television lower third with precomps and null objects

In this segment, we will learn about precomps. This is a very important part of After Effects. It helps you to create complex animations quickly. Once you understand it, we will be able to create a lower third project with more complex layers.

Designing with storyboards

An important part of this book is knowing how to design strong compositions. In this chapter, you will create a lower third. Let's now walk through how this project is designed. In designing any project, the ideation stage is really important; it is when you're generating ideas and developing concepts for the project. It's very important to stay organized during the idea-generating phase. I use Adobe Bridge for this. You can bring in photos and videos, and organize them in Adobe Bridge. You can also label and organize them in a variety of ways.

All design projects have parameters. Ask yourself what the criteria are for your project. When you're creating a project, it's important to know your audience and know where your video will be seen. This will help you to design a project that is appropriate for your audience. Bear this in mind, particularly when you are choosing fonts, colors and images. Ask yourself: is the design legible?

The following screenshot shows a storyboard; you can use this to plan out your ideas for your project. It can be a very basic storyboard to help you organize and plan your project. When you design your storyboard, you have an opportunity to see whether your typography and images work well together. You need to make sure that your designs are readable and can be communicated effectively:

Adobe Bridge

Refer to the following link to find out more about television lower thirds:
`https://www.jbistudios.com/blog/lower-thirds-chyrons-subtitles-dubbing-video-translation`.

Editing masks and using precomps

Let's begin our television lower third. Look at the following screenshot; this is what we're creating. We are creating the `6:30` portion of this project right now:

Final image

To begin with, we are going to create a **compostion (comp)** with solid layers and edit those solid layers with masking techniques, as follows:

1. Create a new 1920 x 1080 comp with a frame rate of `29.97`.

2. Make the comp 9 seconds—`0:00:09:00`. Name it `pattern`.

3. Go to **Layer** | **New** | **Solid**, and change the color to blue.

4. Create a circle shape using the ellipse tool.

5. Drag another ellipse on to the comp layer.

6. Choose a subtract mask:

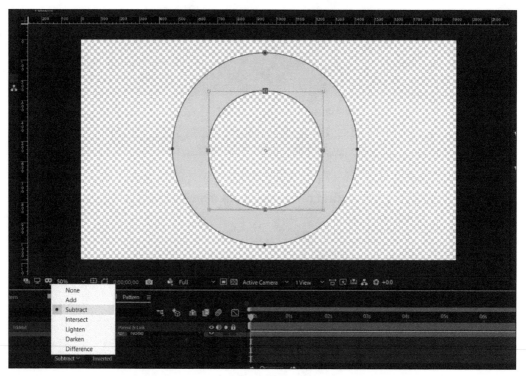

Subtract mask

7. This will allow you to cut out a shape inside your first mask.

8. Choose the Pan Behind Tool. This will allow to move your anchor point, and you can transform around this point.

9. Scale down the layer.

10. Move it up into the top-left corner.

11. Duplicate this layer.

12. Reposition this layer as seen in the following example:

13. Repeat this process until you have at least six circle shapes in your composition.

Just like Photoshop, you can put a variety of assets in one folder in After Effects. In After Effects, this is called precomposing. It's a simple process to precompose something. However, the concept behind it is a little more complicated. The way to precompose the objects in our scene is to have a transparent background and select everything in your composition.

Go to the **Layer** tab in the top-left panel of the screen and choose the **Pre-compose...** option:

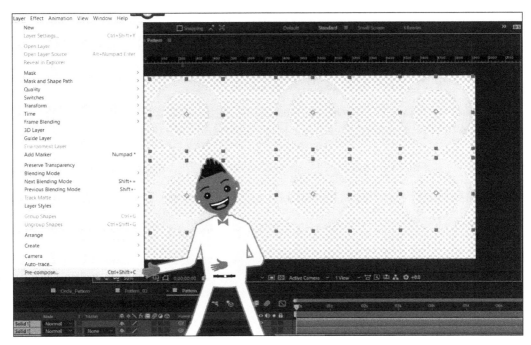

Pre-comp 1

When you precompose something, you get a dialog box. This gives you the option to name your precomp. Choose the option to move all of your attributes into the new composition, as demonstrated in the following screenshot:

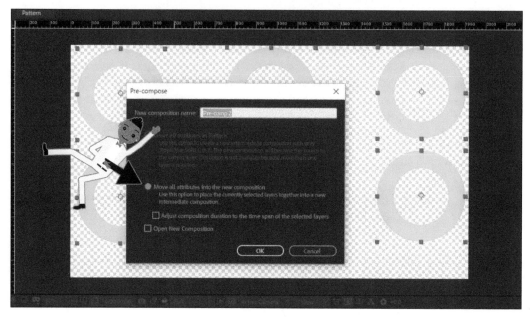

Pre-comp 2

Nesting precomps and using the pen tool

Let's create a background for your shapes, as follows:

- Go to the top-left panel and choose **Layer | New | Solid**
- Move this new **Solid** layer to the bottom of your composition layer
- Next, create a main comp in which to move all of your assets

After creating a new composition, name it Main comp, and then we can apply the same settings as we did in our first comp.

To move a precomp into another composition, simply locate the precomp in your project window and drag it down into your Main comp:

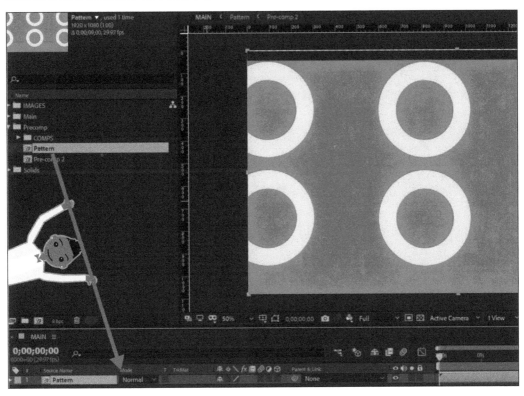

Dragging the precomp

Now, you should see one precomp in your Main comp. Let's adjust this precomp further. Select your pen tool, as demonstrated in the following screenshot:

Pen tool

We will use the pen tool to mask out a shape on your precomp. To use the pen tool, you simply select the layer you want to use the pen tool on. In this case, it's the precomp. Click the pen icon at the desired starting point of your mask.

Move your pen tool to the next desired point, and click again. When you're ready to close the shape, hover near the point you want to close it at. You'll see a small circle icon near the pen tool, meaning that you can close the shape. When you've completed masking this precomp, it should look like the following screenshot:

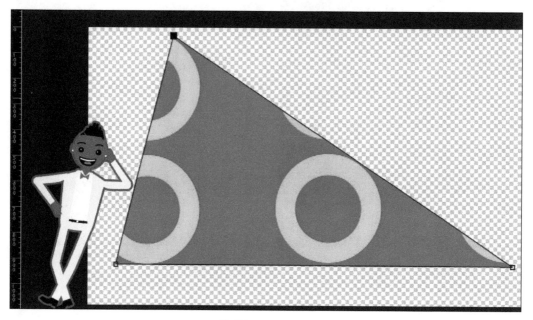

Masking a precomp

Next, I will create another composition for the additional shapes that I will use for my lower third. Create a new composition with the same dimensions and time length as our previous comp. I am essentially going to repeat the exact same process that I did with the previous shapes I created. This time, however, I'm going to use the rectangle tool to make some shapes.

With these new shapes, we won't be using the subtraction mask feature. We're making a series of rectangle shapes and organizing them to create a pattern, as shown in the following screenshot:

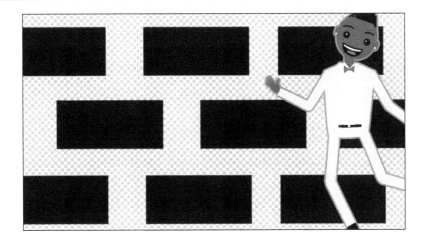

Creating a rectangle pattern

Next, we are going to precompose these new shapes using the following steps:

1. Simply select all the rectangle shapes and choose composition precompose. When you precompose something, a dialog box appears. This gives you options to name your precomp.

2. Choose the **Move all attributes into the new composition** option.

3. The next step is to create a background for your shapes. Go to **Layer | New | Solid**, and make the color yellow.

Since this will be the background for our design, you need to move this new **Solid** layer to the bottom of the stacking order.

Now that you have a new design, you need to move it into the Main comp. The steps for moving a precomp into your Main comp are as follows:

1. Navigate to the Main composition in your project folder. Double-click on Main comp.

2. Find the precomp in your Precomp folder and drag it into the Main comp.

It's very important to stay organized at this point because it will be easy for you to identify where all of your precomps are. When you make a new comp that's not the Main comp, put it into the Precomp folder immediately. The only composition that should be in your Main comp folder is the main composition. This is the composition that you intend to export/render.

Repeat the same process as before, and use the pen tool to mask off around the design in the `Main` comp:

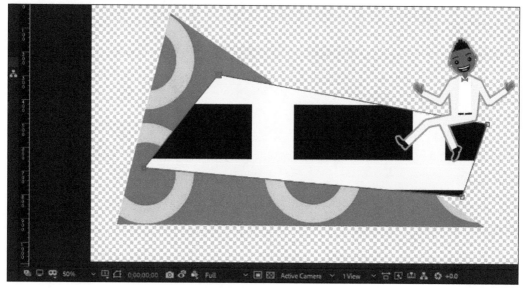

Masking the second pattern

Animations, nulls, text, and rendering

In this section, we will learn how to animate using **Null** objects. We will also learn about rendering our projects.

Parenting and Null object animations

Now, we are going to animate our designs. We have created designs that live in the `Precomp` folder. Double-click on the first precomp you made. In this precomp, you have a nested comp and a Solid layer that you made for your background. Select and center the top precomposed shape layer:

1. Press the R button to reveal the **Rotation** parameters
2. Go to the left-side of the panel, and hit the stopwatch for the **Rotation** parameter
3. Move 90 key frames down to the right in the timeline
4. Scrub the **Rotation** parameter

This will automatically create a key frame, as shown in the following screenshot:

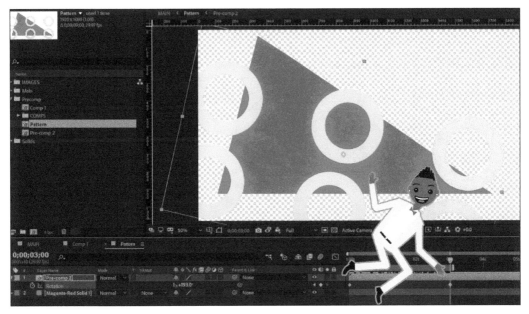

Animation rotation

Go back into the Main comp, and press the spacebar to preview your animation. Give yourself a pat on the back for creating your first animation! Let's animate the next pattern precomp that we created by observing the following steps:

1. In the Main comp, double-click on the remaining pattern precomp.

2. Let's animate this precomp using the same steps that we previously used. We will animate by using the **Position** parameter.

3. Animate this **Pattern** layer so that it's moving to the right.

4. Hit P for **Position**.

5. Go to the beginning of the timeline.

6. Hit the **Position** stopwatch.

7. Go down the timeline 90 key frames.

8. Scrub the **Position** parameter.

You should see the rectangle shapes moving to the right, as seen in the following screenshot:

Animation position

Let's jump back to the Main comp and preview our animation. Press the spacebar to preview our work:

1. In the Main comp, let's import a 1920 x 1080 image to use for our background in the lower third project

2. Drag the background image into the Main comp

3. Bring this image to the bottom layer in the timeline

4. Re-scale the image, if necessary

Parenting null animations

Another animation technique that I want to introduce you to is called parenting animation. Through the process of parenting, any layer you parent to another layer will follow the movement or animation of that layer. In the process of parenting, you will have a parent and a child. A child is anything that is connected to, or parented by, the parent. The child is able to move freely. However, it will always be connected and thus move with the parent. Using a parenting animation, we can create a complex secondary animation. We are going to parent our two shape layers to a **Null** object. The **Null** object is a layer that is essentially invisible. However, this **Null** object can be animated and things can be parented to it.

The following are the steps to create a parenting animation:

1. Create a **Null** object by going up to the **Layer** tab and choose a new **Null** object.

2. Select the two precomped animated patterns.

3. Look to the right of the layers for the **Parent & Link** tab. Look for the coil icon.

4. Click and drag on the coil icon (this is called pick whip).

5. Pick whip this coil to the **Null** object, as demonstrated in the following screenshot:

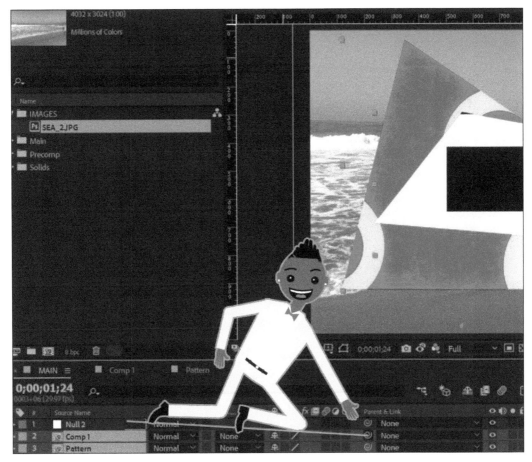

Parenting

Parenting

After parenting these objects to the **Null** object, you will see the word **Null** in the **Parent & Link** tab for both of these layers. This means that these layers will move where the null moves. Just like any layer, this null will animate along the anchor point. That's the first thing we want to adjust. Make sure it's in the correct center position. Use the **Null** object to scale down both precomps. Hit S for the scale parameter and scale the objects down. Move the objects to the lower area of the composition, as seen in the following screenshot. Position the objects in a layout that is similar to the following screenshot. You can position the objects by selecting them on the composition window or you can hit P for Position and scrub the **Position** parameter in the timeline. You can also adjust each object's scale independent of the **Null** object. Adjust your masks for your precomps if necessary. The adjusting of these objects doesn't affect the parenting relationship. As stated earlier, the children are parented and obey the parent, but they are free to move on their own:

Adjusting the mask

Positioning a lower third

Now, we are going to create a basic shape with no animation on it. You will have two precomps with animated shapes on it and one solid layer without any shapes on it.

Creating a dark blue solid layer

In this project, we are building our lower thirds from solid layers. We will add another **Solid** layer to our project and use the **Parenting** tool to connect it to our **Null** object, as follows:

1. Use the pen tool to create a triangle shape.

2. Adjust the **Position** parameter of your object further.

3. Move this new object to beneath the two shapes. Adjust the mask for this **Solid** layer and reposition it, if necessary.

4. Parent this object to the **Null** object.

5. Select the triangle shape and look to the right of the layer for the **Parent & Link** tab. Look for the coil icon.
   Click and drag on the pick whip coil.

6. Pick whip this coil to the **Null** object, as demonstrated in the following screenshot:

Using the pick whip

The triangle pick whip

Now that we have all our objects parented to the **Null** object, we can animate them. Let's animate our lower third onto the screen using the null object, as follows:

1. Select the **Null** object.

2. Hit P for **Position**.

3. Move down in the timeline about 30 key frames.

4. Trim your work area to this point (hit N).

5. Hit the **Position** stopwatch for the **Null** object.

6. Move back to the beginning of the timeline.

7. Select the **Null** object.

8. Scrub the **Null** object **Position** parameter so that the lower third is moving off screen.

9. Moving this at an angle, you will see a motion path line proceeding at a diagonal angle, as demonstrated in the following screenshot. Preview your animation:

The position of an animation null object

Now that you have your objects moving on the screen, you are going to create a secondary animation. We are going to animate the children of the parented object independently. Creating this type of offset movement will enhance the visual interest of the object, and is executed as follows:

1. Go 10 key frames after the last key frame of the **Null** object in the timeline.

2. Select one of the precomped objects on the far left-hand side of the screen.

3. Hit P for the **Position** parameter.

4. Hit the **Position** stopwatch.

5. Go about 10 key frames down from the first key frame.

6. Animate the shape going off screen at an angle, as demonstrated in the following screenshot.

7. Preview your animation, as follows:

Animating the first object at an angle

This will create an offset animation for the object. A motion path shows the direction that your object is taking. If you notice when you animate the position of an object, a motion path appears in the composition window. This path is a dotted line, called a motion path. Apply this offset animation technique to the other solid shape. Motion paths are important for understanding your movement and timing. Timing is everything in animation. One way to control the speed of your animation is where your key frames are in the timeline. You can adjust your key frames by selecting them and sliding them in the timeline. Your key frames should look similar to the following screenshot:

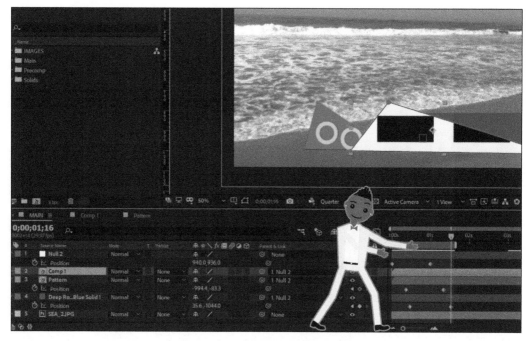

An offset animation for the additional object

Color correction and adjusting masks

We are going to change some of the colors of our shapes. When I discovered all the color correction tools available in After Effects, I swear I did a little dance! These color correction tools are non-destructive, so you can change them at any time. Many of these tools are also available in Photoshop. So, if you're familiar with color correction in Photoshop, some of these tools and concepts will be familiar to you. As you color correct, think of yourself as a colorist using color to help convey some emotion. We are also going to fine-tune our mask shapes. Remember, your precomps and masks are always editable.

Adjusting colors

To edit the color of the yellow triangle shape, you can double-click on the precomp in the timeline, as follows:

1. Select the bottom yellow layer

2. Go to the **Effect & Presets** panel

3. Type `fill`

4. Double-click the **Fill** effect

This will add the effect to whatever you have chosen. As you can see, you get an **Effects** panel that pops up next to your project panel. The default color for this effect is red. Adjust your color by selecting the **Color** box and selecting a new color:

Fill effect

Now go back to your `Main` comp. You will see your background is a different color. Spend some time adjusting the colors of your shapes and background. Use the same **Fill** effect on anything you want to change the color of. You want your text for your lower thirds to stand out from the background of these shapes.

In After Effects, you have access to many image editing tools that come with Photoshop. We're going to use one called **Curves**:

1. Select your photo background layer.

2. Find the effect called **Curves** in the **Effects & Preset** panel.

3. Click on this effect to add it to your photo layer.

4. Look at the **Effect Controls** panel next to your project window.

5. Adjust your curve effects using the bottom button called **Auto**:

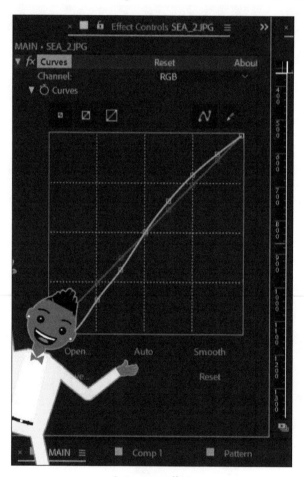

Auto curve effect

6. Next, we will add a photo filter effect to our image. Find this in the effect panel by typing `photo filter`. Double-click and add this effect to your layer. This effect will give your image an overall color effect. Choose a nice cooling filter (such as `80`).

Adjusting masks

You can also adjust the masks of your shape in the `Main` comp window. Remember to edit individual points for your mask by choosing the selection tool and clicking once on one mask path point. Once you see the point filled in (as in the following screenshot), that means it's ready to be edited. If you study the following screenshot, you will see that only one point is filled in. The other two points are empty. This demonstrates how to edit your mask points:

Editing single mask points

You can also add points to your masks by selecting the pen tool, and hovering over the mask where you want to make the point. You will see a + sign. Click on the mask to make an additional point. After adding a mask point, drag this point to the desired location to edit the mask shape:

Pen tool editing path

You are now going to add your show information for your lower third object.

Creating text, easy easing key frames, and rendering

Imagine yourself getting very close to the finish line! We are almost done with this lower third project. You should be very proud of yourself. In this next section, we are going to add some information for our show, using the type tool. Pay special attention to the text tool. It's one of the main communication devices used with After Effects, and is one of the principal means of communicating information. It's very important that you understand how to use this tool. We are also going to learn ways of how to further edit your key frames for more natural movement. Then, we are going to learn a couple of ways of how to render our movie.

The type tool

The type tool is one of the most versatile tools in After Effects. Text layers are useful for many purposes, including lower thirds, animated titles, and dynamic typography. You can fully edit your text layers, spacing, size, and stroke. You can animate the text layers, or the color, size, and position. There's also a complete set of tools for animating your text in complex ways. Creating dynamic typography sets this program apart from any other.

You can add text to your composition using the text tool, as follows:

1. We will begin by selecting the type tool in the top tool panel.

2. Next, click on your comp to add a type to the `Main` comp. This immediately creates a text layer in your composition. Make sure that your type layer is on top of all your other layers.

3. Look to the left-hand side of the screen, and you will find some of your type tool options.

4. You can change the color of your type by selecting the fill color option; this is the box found to the right of your font option.

5. To adjust the scale of your text, hit the S shortcut for scale, and adjust this as you would any other layer:

Type color fill

The type fill

Spend time creating individual text layers for your show information. Use one shape for the day of your show. Use another one for the time of your show. And finally, include the name of your show on one of the shapes. We will go over more of these type tools, but for now, just adjust your type so that it fits in all of the shapes, as demonstrated in the following screenshot:

Adjusting the type

Adjusting the text

Now, you will parent your text to the shape you have it positioned inside of. Your text should move with the shapes it is positioned in. Go to a point in your timeline where all your animation has happened, and the lower third is completely in place and framed correctly.

Follow this up by selecting each line of text and parent it to the corresponding object. You parent your text with these steps:

1. Select the text layer and use the pick whip tool
2. Drag the coil tool to the appropriate shape

Animation is basically making things move across time. After Effects gives you the ability to control how things move in-between frames. Understanding how to control how things move will make your animation look natural. One way to do this is to ease your key frames. This is an advanced topic that we will cover in much greater detail in future chapters.

The first step to learning key frames is the understanding of the selection tool. In order to master it, go to the timeline and click and drag a square around all your key frames. The following screenshot demonstrates how to select your key frames:

Selecting key frames

Our next task is to ease our key frames. Editing your key frames is crucial to create smooth movements:

1. Right-click on the key frames
2. Choose the **Keyframe Assistant** option
3. Select **Easy Ease**

The following screenshot demonstrates how to access the **Keyframe Assistant** panel:

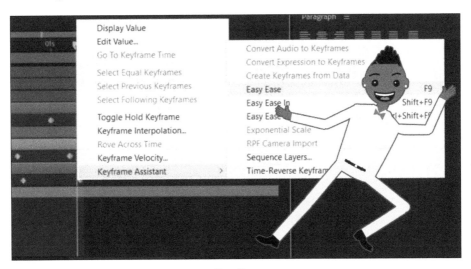

Easy Ease

Remember to always ease your key frames. Take a look at the following screenshot to see how eased key frames should look:

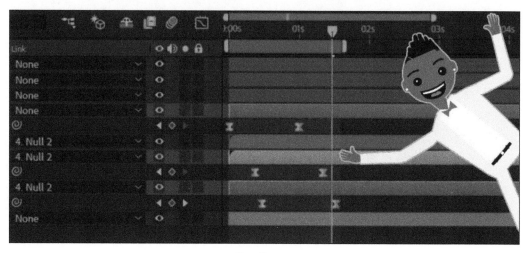

Easy Ease 2

Rendering options

Lower thirds are typically used for television shows and placed on top of video footage. In order to place footage on video, the composition needs to have a transparent background. Rendering is how we can create a video of your projects. If you want to render your lower third by itself, perform the following steps on a transparent background:

1. Go to the Main composition
2. Turn off everything except the lower third
3. Add to the render queue
4. Choose **Lossless**
5. Choose the **QuickTime** format
6. Choose RGB + Alpha
7. Navigate to the folder you want to save it in
8. Name your video

 Your render should only be the length of your project. Check the last frame of your project before you render it so that you don't have any blank frames.

You can also render your project using Adobe Media Encoder. I recommend rendering this way, particularly if you don't need your video on a transparent background. You can work in After Effects while you're rendering in Adobe Media Encoder. You need to be sure that Adobe Media Encoder is downloaded to your computer:

1. Go to composition.
2. Choose **Add to Adobe Media Encoder**.
3. In Adobe Media Encoder, you should see your project.
4. You should see **h264** under your title. If not, find it in the drop-down menu.
5. Hit the **h264** icon.
6. The **Export settings** option should come up.
7. Go to basic video settings.
8. Adjust the target bitrate/maximum bitrate to about five or lower (small numbers = a smaller file size; bigger numbers = a bigger file size). Notice that the estimated file size at the bottom of this screen goes down when you adjust the target bitrate.
9. Choose the green start button triangle in the top-right corner of the screen.

Summary

In this chapter, we learned more about **Solid** layers, masking, key frames, the **Keyframe Assistant**, the text tool, **Null** objects, precomps, and how to create a lower third for a television show. We also learned about easy ease and how to render your projects. After reading this chapter, you can group your layers into precomps and edit masks. This is crucial as we move forward into the next chapter, where we will design with shape layers and work more with editing and animating masks. We will build on the skills that we have learned from this chapter and learn about shape layers, text presets, editing audio, and how to create an animated lyric video for social media.

Questions

1. What is a pen tool and how do you use it to create custom masks?
2. How do you adjust your key frames?
3. What is the **Keyframe Assistant**?
4. What is easy ease?
5. How do you activate the text tool?
6. How do you use **Null** objects?
7. How do you create precomps?

3

Using Shape Layers to Create an Animated Lyric Video

In this chapter, we are going to work with shape layers. Shape layers are like solid layers, except they are much more powerful! Essentially, shape layers are a bit like Illustrator, you can create custom shapes and edit them, but you have access to tons of animation parameters as well. Shape layers are a natural continuation of solid layers and the masking that we did in the last chapter. Both solid layers and shape layers are vector objects. They can be scaled infinitely without losing quality.

We will use shape layers as transition elements in our project. Every time you create an animation project, ask yourself, is there a creative way I can transition in or out of this scene? By the end of this chapter, you will know a couple interesting ways to transition between your scenes.

The following topics will be covered in this chapter:

- Shape layer animation
- Mask animation
- Editing audio
- Text animation

Using shape layers to create transitions and background graphics

In this shape layer project, we will duplicate and reuse a lot of elements. We will change the color of the shapes and offset the key frames for complex animated designs. This project will get your feet wet with shape layers; however, there are more advanced features with shape layers that we won't cover. Please feel free to explore after I have introduced the shape layer concept.

We are building a looping lyric video for a fictional children's movie. These types of videos are used on social media to generate excitement about a song or a movie. Understanding how to animate typography in a kinetic way is important in the field of motion graphics. Moving typography helps convey your message in a more entertaining way than static type. Let's get started with shape layers.

Creating shape 1

The interface for shape layers can be found in two areas: at the top of the interface in the tool panel, and also in the timeline:

1. Go to **Layer** | **New** | **Shape Layer** | **Add** | **Ellipse**.

2. Name it Circle 1.

3. Twirl down the **Ellipse Path 1**.

4. Increase the size to 1000.

5. Go to **Add** | **Stroke**.

6. Increase the stroke width to 90:

Stroke width

Add a solid-color background:

1. Go to **Add | Trim Paths**.

2. Go to **Start | 100**.

3. Go to the beginning of the timeline and click the stop watch.

4. Go to key frame 20 and set the start parameter to 0.

5. Hit the *N* shortcut to trim your work area.

6. Hit *Spacebar* to preview, and, with that, you've created your first shape layer animation!

7. Open the shape layer.

8. Increase the stroke width size.

9. Duplicate the shape layer.

10. Right-click this layer.

11. Rename your circle layer 2.

12. Twirl down content | **Stroke 1**.

13. Change the stroke color:

Stroke color

14. Go to **Stroke 1 | Stroke width**.

15. Reduce the stroke width to 30.

16. So these paths will animate on at different times, go to **Trim path | Start | Offset keyframes**:

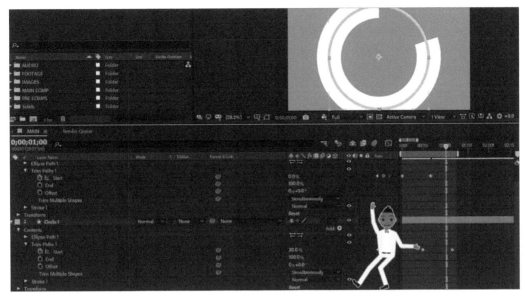

Offset key frames

Select your key frames for the trim path. Drag the key frames so they are offset. Look at the offset key frames I am pointing to in the preceding screenshot:

1. Rename Circle 1 to `Thick line`

2. Rename Circle 2 to `Thin line`

3. Duplicate Thick line

4. Move to the top

5. Change the stroke color of `Thick line 2`

Next, look closely at the **Stroke 1** option. Under the **Stroke 1** options is **Dashes**. Slowly look to the right of **Dashes** and you will see **+** and **-**, which are called **Dashes**. Clicking on the **+** will allow you to add dashes to your object:

1. Across from **Dashes**, find the **+** and **-** signs.

2. Hit the **+** sign twice. Under **Dashes**, you have three parameters called **Dash**, **Gap**, and **Offset**.

3. Adjust the gaps to `120`:

Gap parameters

4. Increase the Gap to `120`.

    Offset the key frames for the trim path so these elements will be animated at different times. Remember, timing is everything in animation. You want these key frames offset so each animation happens a few key frames behind the offset key frames.

5. Adjust the stroke width to `500` for **Thick line 2**.

Creating a new polystar shape layer

We need you to create a new transition shape layer. This will help us transition to our next scene in a creative way:

1. Create a new shape layer.

2. Add a **Polystar** shape to our layer:

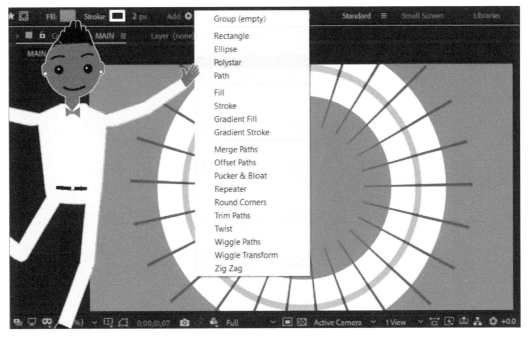

Polystar shape

Add a **Polystar** shape to the empty shape layer. By default, when you add a shape layer to your project, it's empty. You have to add any shapes you want to see. You can add items to your shape layer in the timeline to the right of the contents tab, or you can add them with the bar in the top right:

1. Add a fill.

2. Twirl down the polystar.

3. Add 30 points:

Add points

4. Next, expand the outer radius to 1250.

5. Go to the last key frame of your animation and create a key frame for the outer radius.

6. Go to the mid point where your circles are half way through their animations.

7. Make your outer radius 0.

8. At that same point in the timeline, hit the stop watch for your inner radius.

9. Jump to the last key frame and expand you inner radius to 1080.

10. Spend some time offsetting your inner radius key frames to achieve the following screenshot:

Inner/outer radius

Creating a transition shape

We are going to add our final transition shape for shape 1.

Now you need to go to the point in the timeline where the last shape is almost fully covering the screen. See the following screenshot:

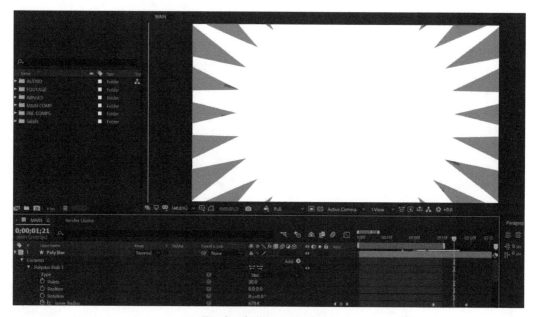

Timeline location new shape

To create a transition animated shape, follow these steps:

1. Create a new shape layer.
2. Name this layer `Transition` stroke.
3. Add an ellipse.
4. Add a stroke.
5. Change the color of the stroke.
6. Twirl down the contents of the transition stroke layer.
7. Find **Ellipse Path 1**.
8. Animate the ellipse by changing its size, scaling it up and eventually having it leave the scene.

9. Go to the first key frame for the size change.

10. Add a key frame for the stroke width.

11. Go to the last size key frame, choose the stroke parameter, and increase the stroke width so that on that frame your stroke looks like the following screenshot:

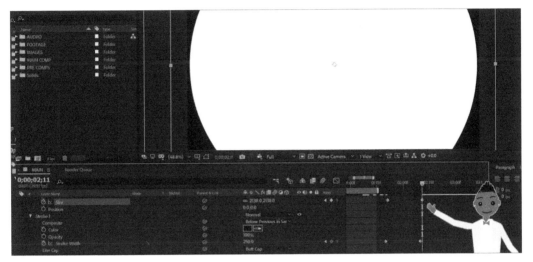

Circle 2 transition stroke width

We are using this shape to reveal the character underneath. We have already created the animated mask shapes. We are now going to use an additional mask to cut out the center of the polygon shape:

1. Choose the last shape layer created.

2. At the top of the toolbar, select the ellipse tool.

3. To the far right, next to the star shape, choose the **Tool Creates Mask** tool:

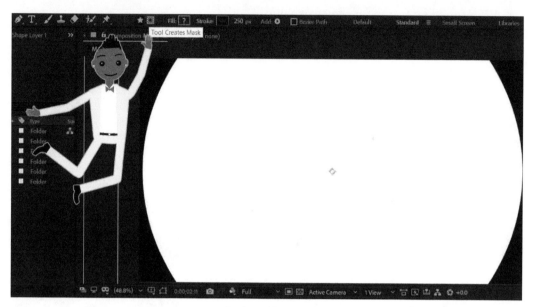

Tool creates mask

Use this tool to click and drag to make a shape to cut through this mask shape:

1. Put your mouse in the center of this shape.

2. Press *Ctrl +Shift* to constrain this shape. This will create a perfect mask shape. Starting the shape from the center will perfectly center it. Look at the new mask created on the polystar layer.

3. Click invert to cut out the center of the shape:

Invert

When you click on the Invert option, it makes your mask invert. This will effectively cut through your mask. The following screenshot demonstrates how you can see the background through the cut-out shape:

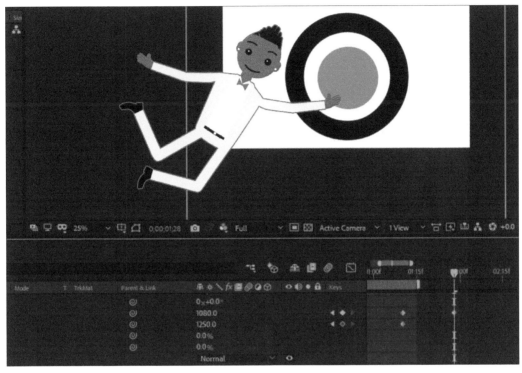

Cut out

We need to animate this mask and have the animation aligned with the key frames from the transition stroke layer. This will ensure the mask animation is in sync with the transition stroke layer:

1. Go to the first key frame of the transition stroke layer.
2. Select the mask on the polystar layer.
3. Create a key frame for the mask.
4. Go to the last key frame of the transition stroke layer.

5. Adjust the mask so it animates off the screen with the transition stroke mask. To select all mask points, double-click one mask shape until you get the mask bounding box. This will allow you to adjust your mask and keep the perfect ellipse shape:

Mask bounding box

The first key frame mask shape will be so small that it's barely noticeable. Key frame the last mask so that it completely fill the screen.

This process is called **creating a wipe transition**. This is used frequently in motion graphics to transition in and out of scenes. Since this is a circular shape, this transition would be called a **radial wipe**. We need to trim the other shape layers except the transition layer, background layer, and the polystar layer:

1. Go to the first key frame of the polystar layer mask layer.

2. Select all layers except the background, the polystar layer, and the transition stroke layer.

3. Trim your layers. Press *Alt +]* or press and hold Shift and drag your layers to the left.

Pressing *Shift* will snap your layers to where your time indicator is parked. Make sure you see the trim icon.

Importing audio, text animation presets, and background graphics

We are going to finish the lyric video by adding music, creating dynamic animated typography, and creating an animated background.

Importing audio and creating composition markers

You import audio layers the same way you import anything. An audio layer is just like any other layer, except it doesn't have some transform properties. Any layer that is represented by a visual image will have position, scale, and rotation transform properties. However, an audio layer isn't represented visually; therefore, you don't have any of the usual transform properties. You will have access to wave forms that will display the sound variations on your audio layers.

To reveal your wave form, simply do the following:

1. Twirl down the audio layer to reveal the wave forms:

Audio

These audio layers have volume that can be animated.

2. To adjust and key frame your audio volume, reveal the stopwatch audio parameter.

3. Key frame the audio levels in the negative direction. You can tell when your audio has zeroed out because the waveform will be a flat line. You have audio controls on any layer that has an audio track:

Audio keyframing

4. Next, we are going to listen to our audio and listen for the lyrics to make composition markers for our text. To add a composition marker, hit *Shift* and press a number:

The composition marker

This will create a marker on your composition with a marker on it. You can further edit that marker by double-clicking on the number. This will reveal a panel that lets you rename the number. Here, you can enter notes for your layer. Double-click that number to add the name of your lyric:

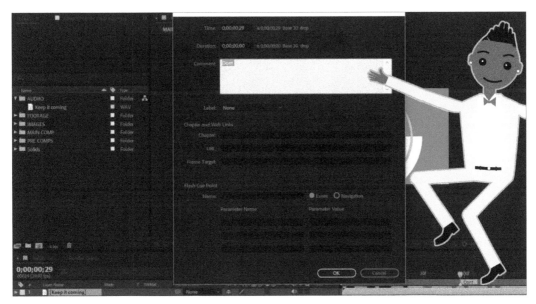

Renaming the marker

Keep doing this until you have about 10 seconds of music with the lyrics notated in the markers.

Text animators

Kinetic typography is an essential tool to understand in motion graphics. Luckily, we have access to lots of text presets that provide us with instant animation. Go to **Effects & Presets** and twirl down **Animation Presets | Text | Organic | Drop Bounce**:

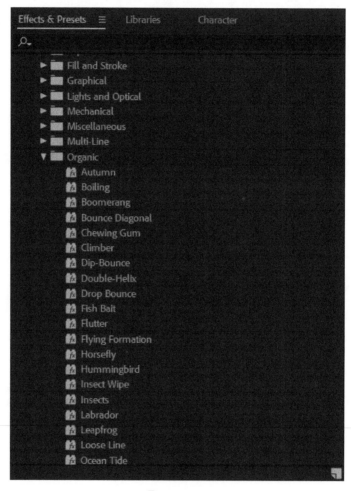

Text presets

While one of your lines of type is selected, double-click on the **Drop Bounce** preset. It will automatically add this preset to your text.

Make sure you have enough room for your first line of type to be animated. Adjust your layers if necessary:

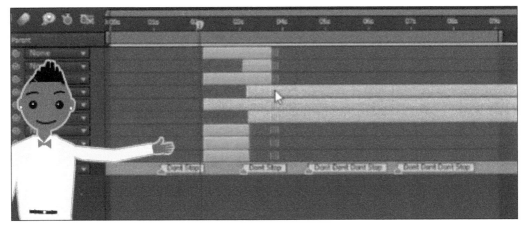

Adjusting layers

We are going to use the type tool to type in the first text. Go to the point in the timeline with your first marker with the lyrics. Type the first word of the lyric. Type the second word in the lyrics on a separate line. You should have one text layer per word in your lyrics. Center your text in the screen and scale it down, as shown in the following screenshot:

Centering text

Select the second layer of text. Ensure that the text matches the audio. Choose another animation preset. Look in the animation folder. Next, go to the point in the timeline when the next line of lyrics needs to be animated. Animate off your type. Look in the animate off presets and click on one of these presets to animate off your text.

Editing your text preset key frames

The text presets don't always look exactly how you want them after adding them to your text. Therefore, you may need to edit the preset key frames:

1. Press *U* to reveal the key frames that create the preset.

2. Select all key frames and hit the *Alt* key on Windows, or the option key on macOS.

3. Drag your key frames. This will adjust all your key frames relative to each other. Or, you can select the key frames and move them individually.

Bringing your key frames closer together makes your animation happen faster, while moving them further apart makes the animations move slower:

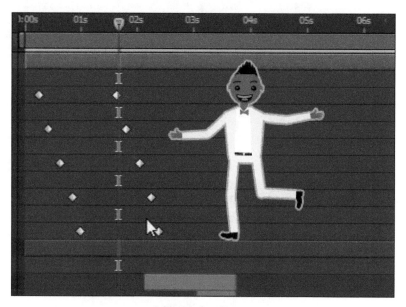

Adjusting key frames

Adding a layer style to your text is done as follows:

1. Go to **Layer | Layer Styles | Stroke**.

2. Next, you can adjust the stroke color:

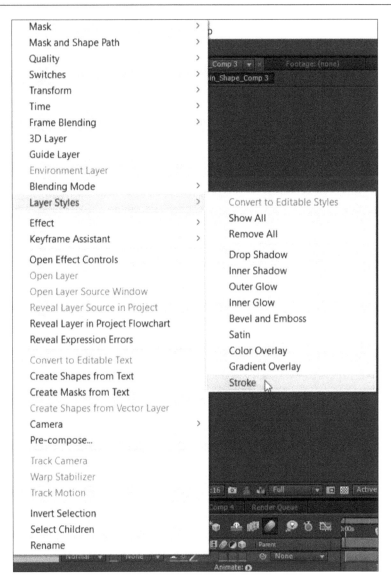

Adjusting the stroke

Make sure your text layers are at the top of your stacking order. Things should happen in this order:

1. The shape layers animate on and off with the text.

2. The transition happens, revealing a character.

3. Repeat *step 1* as many times as needed for your lyrics:

Transition

To make sure your layers are in the correct order, follow these steps:

1. Select your all your text layers.

2. Move all text underneath your other layers.

Creating an animated background shape

We are going to animate a repeating background element for our animation. We are going to duplicate the radial dash line layer:

1. Adjust the key frames for this layer so it animates on and off with the text.

2. This needs to be underneath the text, as shown in the following screenshot:

We are going to make this project a square format for better viewing on social media. Go to **Composition | Composition Setting** and make the composition size 1,080 x 1,080.

Summary

In this chapter, we learned about the powerful and complex world of shape layers. We learned how to create custom shapes, edit them, and create animation with these shapes. We learned how to use shape layers as transition elements in our projects. We also learned about the exciting world of text animation presets. We learned how to animate in and out of text animation. Remember—text presets are the starting point for kinetic typography. Play with these parameters to get unique animations. You don't want your animations to be too predictable and look as though they came directly from a preset. Alter the text presets to create something unique.

Questions

1. What are layer styles?
2. How do you access layer styles?
3. What are shape layers?
4. What is a transition?
5. How do you create a composition marker?
6. What are waveforms?
7. What is a text preset?
8. How do you access text presets?

Further reading

Consult the following pages for more information on the topics in this chapter:

- Saving presets: `https://helpx.adobe.com/after-effects/using/effects-animation-presets-overview.html`
- Social media file formats: `https://sproutsocial.com/insights/social-media-image-sizes-guide/`

4
Creating an Infographic with Character Animator

In this chapter, we will bring together all the things we have learned so far. We will continue building on the topics we've covered so far by creating an information-based project, jumping into the exciting world of character animation! We will rely heavily on assets from Illustrator. Artwork from Illustrator is vector-based and can be scaled. **Adobe Character Animator** and **Illustrator** must be installed on your machine to follow along with this lesson.

The following topics will be covered in this chapter:

- Kinetic typography
- Creative transitions
- Character animation
- Icon animation

Technical requirements

You need Photoshop, Illustrator installed and a web camera.

Infographics

Infographics are video projects that can be used to communicate information in exciting and memorable ways. Motion graphics animation tools are uniquely suited to this type of storytelling. The ability to create kinetic typography and dazzling transitions makes After Effects perfect for creating infographics. For this project, I want you to think of an issue that has factual data you can explain. Alternatively, you can choose to follow along and use the data and character I use, or you could base your project on an interesting article you have read. Another idea would be to create an infographic about a simple fact or food recipe. The important thing is that there is some information to be conveyed in the project. You should limit the amount of text in your project or it will be too overwhelming for viewers to read it. You could also include some subtle background music to help push your narrative along.

Text

In motion graphics, it's important to understand how to set good type so that it's visually pleasing, has a clear message, and is compositionally strong. It's also important to know how to edit your text. The power of well-designed text is used in the creation of film titles, videos, commercials, and animated gifs. Well-designed text can be an art form in itself. Take time to choose just the right font for your project. Consider what's the least amount of text you can put on the screen at a time to convey the information you want to communicate. It's also important to know how to tweak your text so that it's spaced correctly and stands out in its environment. Carefully consider which fonts to use. Color also makes a huge difference to the emotional impact and readability of text. Start looking at text all around you, in print and in the media. What makes text look good? What makes it stand out and be memorable? Try to recreate text treatments to understand the process of creating beautiful text.

We went over text in previous chapters, but in this chapter, let's discuss spacing features. On the far-right of the panel, near the **Effects** panel, we have our **Character** panel. This is where you control your text parameters. Create some text and let's go over these controls. In the top-left corner of the **Character** panel, you have different fonts to choose from. Click on the dropdown to reveal the different fonts installed on your computer:

Fonts

Under the fonts, you have different weights for your font. Click on this to see what weights are available for the font. Typically, you will have access to bold and italicized weights for your fonts.

To the right of the weights, there is a dropdown that provides you with all of the color selection options. This is where you can add a stroke to your font and change the color of it. You can change the font size underneath the font tab:

Font size

This tab is used to adjust the tracking or the spacing between letters. I use this a lot, because text isn't always perfect after typing. Most text needs to have the tracking adjusted:

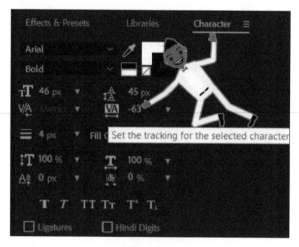

Tracking

This is used to adjust the stroke width:

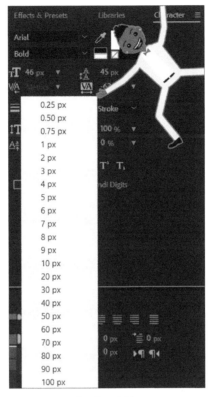

Stroke width

This is used to determine exactly where your stroke is on your type. You have different options, such as **Fill Over Stroke** and **Stroke Over Fill**. Experiment with these to see their differences:

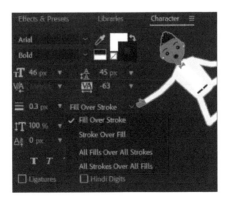

Fill Over Stroke

Under this panel, there is the **Paragraph** panel. This helps you with text alignment:

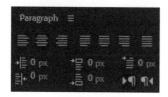

Paragraph

Next, let's look at the **Drop Shadow** feature. **Drop Shadow** is located in the **Effects & Presets** panel. Add this to some text to see what this effect can do. I love this effect; it's so useful and versatile:

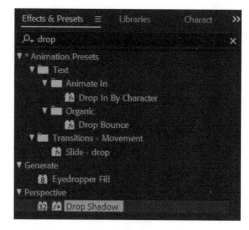

Drop Shadow

Play around with the **Opacity**, the **Distance**, **Direction**, and **Softness** to get comfortable with this tool:

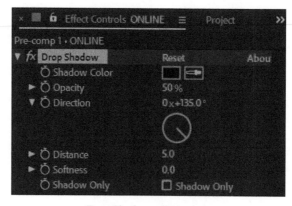

Drop Shadow adjustments

Creating text on a path

Have you seen those videos where text travels along a path? A custom path is a vector path that is drawn freehand using the pen tool in After Effects. In After Effects, you can make your type align with a path and travel along that path!

We can align our text to a path by following these steps:

1. Create your type.

2. Select the text layer.

3. Create a path with the pen tool on the text layer.

4. Twirl down Text.

5. Twirl down Path Options.

6. To the right, choose the path you just created (Mask 1):

Inserting text along a path

Animated text

For this project, we are creating an infographic video. Spend some time looking for some information you want to share in this project. You can also choose to download and use the same files I'm using, to follow along. Create your lines of text on two different layers, as follows:

1. Create some text.

2. Turn on title-safe guides.

3. Make sure the text is centered.

4. Create a background.

5. Create text—ONLINE LEARNING.

6. Turn on continuous rasterized on all layers.

7. Use the following text presets:

    ° Fly in with a twist

    ° Straight in by word

Sometimes, when you select a text preset, you will need to adjust its settings. The text may not animate in the right place. You can adjust your preset starting position in the following way:

- Twirl down **Text**.

- Twirl down **Animator 1**.

- Twirl down **Range Selector 1**.

- Find **Position** and go to the start of the timeline. Adjust **Position** if necessary.

See the following screenshot for the correct **Position** parameter to adjust:

Adjusting preset position

Editing and importing Illustrator files

Understanding how to put your Illustrator artwork on individual layers is critical, because you can animate each of these layers in After Effects. These layers are vectors, so they can be scaled up without losing quality, and can easily be edited. Separating images from the background in Photoshop can be a long process. You can import `ep` files into Illustrator and save them as `ai` files. Make sure Illustrator is downloaded on your computer. Open up a file in Illustrator and let's take a look at layers!

In Illustrator, the layer stacking order is like Photoshop and After Effects; hierarchy is important. What's on the top layer will appear in front of everything else. To arrange these layers, simply select a layer and move it in the stacking order.

Very often, every element of an image will be on one layer. You can separate these and put them on their own layer in Illustrator. To see all of the elements of an image, twirl down **Layers**:

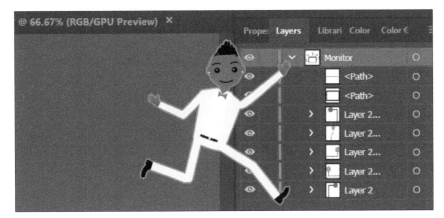

Illustrator twirl down

Creating a new layer in Illustrator

As you can see in this screenshot, there are other elements that make up this image. If you were to import this into After Effects, everything would be on one layer. You would not be able to animate these elements individually, though. Let's take a look at part of the interface of the Illustrator **Layers** panel. Look at the lower-right corner of the Illustrator window. There's a button called **Create New Layer**:

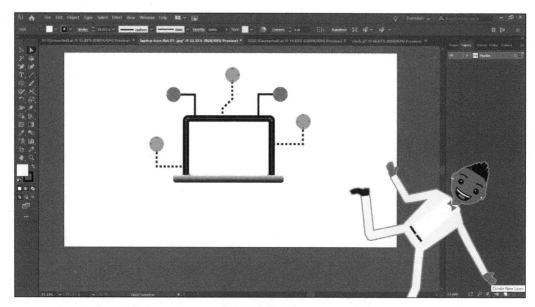

Illustrator new layer

Click on the **Create New Layer** button. This is how you create a new layer in Illustrator.

Once you've created a layer in Illustrator, you need to drag the element you want into that layer. If you double-click on that layer, you can rename it:

Dragging to a new layer

Now that you know how to create separate layers for your illustrations. Take a few moments to drag each element to its own layer. We are going to animate these elements in After Effects later:

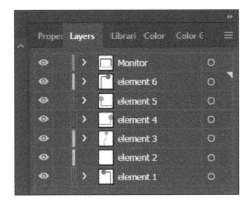

Separate layers

You can edit your Illustrator file extensively. This is great for animation purposes.

The Eyedropper tool

One of my go-to editing tools for changing the color of an element is the Eyedropper tool, which can be used as follows:

1. You use this tool by selecting the element you want to change.

2. Go to the far-left of the Illustrator panel.

3. Choose the **Eyedropper Tool (I)** or the fill icon:

Eyedropper

4. Once you have selected either one of these, you can change the color of the element:

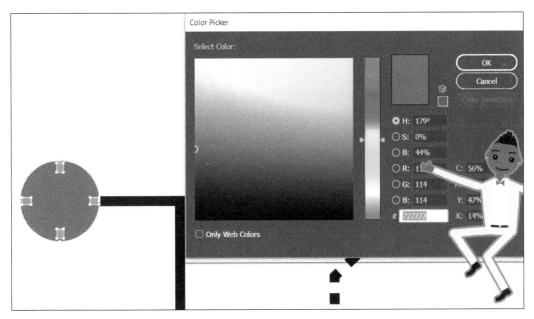

Changing the color of an element

Changing the color of text is done just as it is in After Effects. You can use the Eyedropper tool to choose a color onscreen to change your element to.

5. To save your file, go up to the upper-left corner of the screen and, under the **File** tab, choose **Save As...**:

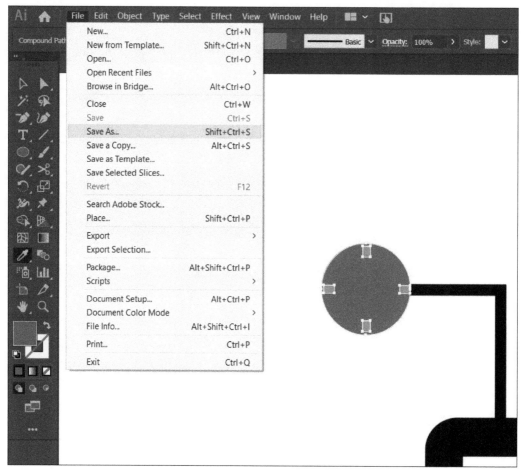

Save

This is where you can save your file in a variety of different formats. For our purposes, we want our illustrations saved as Illustrator files. Choose the Adobe Illustrator *AI file format.

Now jump back to After Effects. Once you import your Illustrator file into After Effects, you can jump back into Illustrator, modify the existing layers, save them, and they will automatically update in After Effects. However, any new layers created in the Illustrator file will not import into After Effects. If you need to add a new layer to an Illustrator file, I recommend you save a new Illustrator file. Import the new Illustrator file and incorporate that new layer into the After Effects project. Now we are ready to import our Illustrator files into After Effect and start animating them! I love this process because Illustrator files are so beautiful and easy to work with. So, the way we import our Illustrator files correctly is by choosing the following options:

1. **Import As: Composition - Retain Layer Sizes**

2. **Import**

Click on **Create a composition**.

Now that you have imported your Illustrator files, you should see a composition automatically appear in the project panel. Move it into your `precomp` folder:

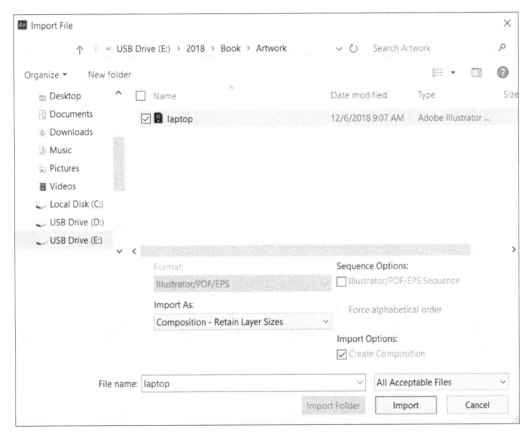

Importing an Illustrator file

This will also import a folder with the individual layers. Move this folder into the IMAGES folder. I love this—it's so organized if you set it up correctly in Illustrator! Take a look at the size of these IMAGES in the folder. This is important because bigger layers increase the render time. Smaller-sized layers are easier to animate. Since these are Illustrator files, they can be scaled up and not lose their quality:

1. Navigate to the Illustrator precomp.

2. Duplicate this so that you have a backup copy in After Effects.

3. Double-click on one of these **PRECOMPS**. You will see your laptop's individual elements set up exactly how we created them in Illustrator.

4. When you import Illustrator files, be sure to turn on continuously rasterize:

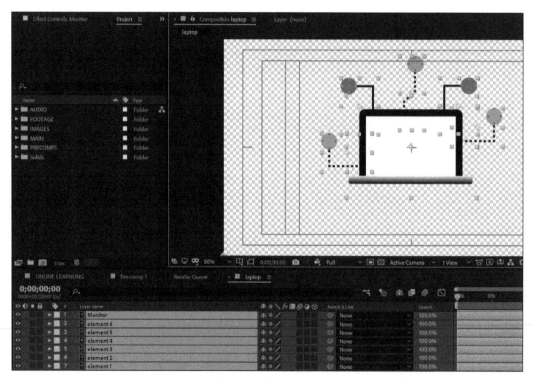

Continuously rasterize

Continuously rasterize is a way to make your layers render in full resolution. Since these are Illustrator files, they will look crisp no matter how much they are scaled up. Now we are going to parent all of our elements to our monitor:

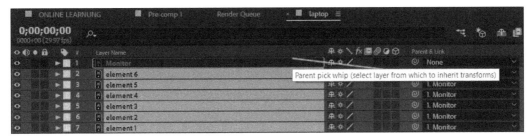

Parent elements

Copy all of these elements and paste them into the composition with your type composition, then do the following:

1. Name this composition ONLINE LEARNING
2. Select the monitor layer you parented everything to
3. Scale this layer down to fit in the scene

When you move this layer, all your elements will move with it, because you parented them to it:

Monitor resize

Let's take a look at what we have created so far and be proud of ourselves! We now have our first logo element set up and ready to be animated. Great job!

Animation principles

At this point, I am going to slow things down and talk about animation principles. We are about to animate our logo and I want you to have a greater understanding of how to move your elements in convincing dynamic ways. Walt Disney — one of the great pioneers of animation — created 12 animation principles that we still use today:

- Timing

- Ease in and out (or slow in and slow out)

- Arcs

- Anticipation

- Exaggeration

- Squash and stretch

- Secondary action

- Follow through and overlapping action

- Straight ahead action and pose-to-pose action

- Staging

- Appeal

- Personality

The ones I want to pay special attention to are timing, ease in and out, secondary action, and personality. Timing is everything in animation. I will repeat this many times in this book. A rule I almost always use is the rule of 10 key frames. It takes the eye about 10 key frames to visually register anything. Make sure you have at least 10 frames between each action. You may need more frames if you have a lot of information on the screen, but this is a good starting point. Take special care in deciding how long something should be onscreen. You do not want the viewer to be bored, so do not let your animations lag. This is something you will get the hang of the more you animate.

The next thing to pay attention to is ease in and out. This is one of the most important things in animating a convincing, elegant action. In the real world, objects need time to accelerate and slow down, like the human body does; most objects move in this way. There's always a gradual easing at the start and end of a movement. To accomplish this in After Effects, we use the Easy Ease key frame assistant. Adding this immediately makes your animation look better.

Secondary actions also add some personality and realism to your animation. Secondary actions are when your objects move into their positions and have a secondary movement after they land there. It isn't necessary to always use secondary movements, but it can add weight and believability to your movements. It also makes your animations imperfect, which generates interest and creates personality. We will go over these principles a lot more in this book.

Animating a monitor

Now let's get to animating our computer monitor:

- Move 10–20 key frames down the timeline after our text appears on the screen
- Move the anchor point of the monitor to the bottom edge of your monitor

To move your anchor point, choose the pan behind tool (Y) and move the anchor point. Now this object will animate around the anchor point. It's important to set this up before animating your object:

Monitor anchor point

At this point, we need to lock our parameters where they are. We do that by creating blank key frames:

- Set scale and rotate key frames at this point
- Move back in the timeline (to the left) 10 key frames

- Scale down the monitor to 0
- Turn on motion blur for everything

Now we are going to create a fake camera move. This will be used as a transition element for our infographic video. We create camera nulls by parenting everything but the background of the null object:

- Go to the point in the timeline after the monitor has been animated.
- Create a null object. Select everything except the background.
- Parent everything selected to the null object.
- Easy ease all of these key frames.
- Turn on motion blur for everything except the background. Remember, motion blur must be turned on in two locations:

Motion blur to icons

Easy Ease will soften your movements and will make them look more organic. Select the key frames for the monitor and the null. Go to **Animation | Keyframe Assistance | Easy Ease**:

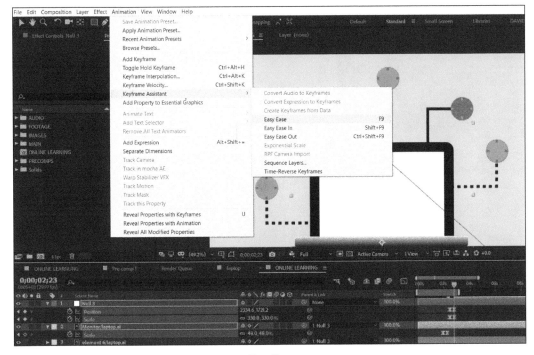

Easy Ease

Now let's animate our fake camera push on our monitor. Here are the steps:

1. Stay at the point where the monitor has been animated.
2. Create a key frame for the scale and position of the null object.
3. Jump down (to the right) 10 key frames.

4. Adjust the **Position** parameter and scale so that the monitor fills the screen:

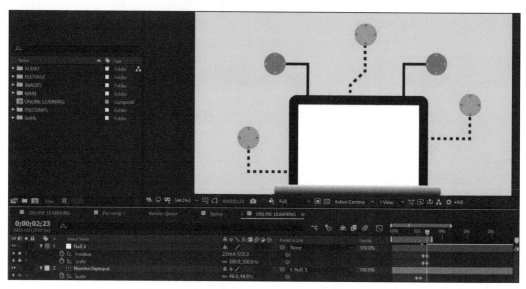

Monitor full screen

Now we are going to animate all of our element pieces. The following are the steps to do that:

1. Go to the point in the timeline where the monitor fills the screen and select all your elements to your monitor.

2. Parent them to your monitor.

3. For each of these elements, position the anchor points at the end of the line.

This will ensure our elements are animating from the correct spot:

Anchor point element

Now that your anchor points and your elements are parented correctly to the monitor, we can start animating them. Here's how we can do that:

1. Select the first element and make a key frame for scale

2. Jump down the timeline 10 key frames (to the right) and set key frames for scale

3. Jump back to the previous scale key frame and scale that element down to 0

Great! Let's preview what we have so far! You should see your animated text on the screen. The next thing you should see is the monitor. Next, you should see your fake camera push in and one of your elements scaling up from the background. (All your elements should be in the background.)

The next step is to create a secondary scale movement. Go to the last key frame position, go 10 key frames to the right, then create a blank key frame.

This is how you create a blank key frame. This is helpful for holding a key frame. Also, you can use these triangles to jump between key frames:

- Jump backward to the keyframe (to the left).

- Scale that key frame up to 120:

Adding a blank key frame

Next, you need to Easy Ease these scale key frames:

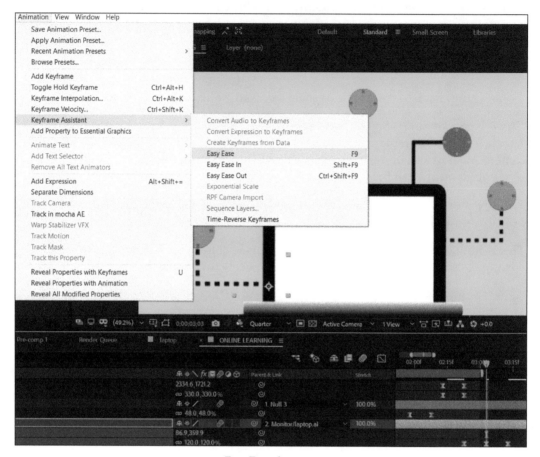

Easy Ease elements

Excellent! Let's look at what we've accomplished. On previewing your work, you should have your monitor element animating on with secondary movement, with motion blur turned on. If turning motion blur on makes your computer run too slowly, you can turn motion blur off temporarily. You will need to remember to turn it back on before you render your project. Repeat the steps to animate the rest of your elements on for your monitor.

At this point, you have all the powerful tools for animating a text with text presets. You also know how to use a camera null. You are grooving along! The next thing we are going to do is animate more type using the same tools we used for the online learning introduction. Be certain that you have time to see the monitor animate on fully with all its pieces and the camera push in. Timing is everything. If you start your text animation too soon, it won't be a pretty sight. Let it rest for a bit, then start animating on the next message. Take a while to animate the text (today's schools are under pressure to do more with less). Be sure to pause in between the lines of text— this will give the viewer time to read it. We are going to add an adjustment layer in between the text and the monitor elements:

1. Go to the **Layer** tab.

2. Then go to **Adjustment Layer**.

3. This will add an adjustment layer to your timeline:

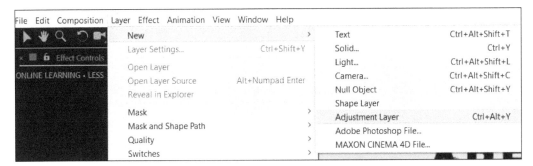

Adjustment layer

Adjustment layers are similar to null objects. They are like a blank layer that you can add effects to and will affect everything underneath them. I'm dropping some important knowledge here; be sure to pick it up and remember it! Effects on an adjustment layer affect everything underneath it in the stacking order. We don't want it to affect the new animated type, so put the adjustment layer under the new type.

Now that we've added our adjustment layer, we can add an effect to it. Here's how we can do that:

Go to the point in the timeline where your monitor and all the elements are completely animated on

1. Go to your effects and add a **Fast Box Blur**

2. While the box radius is at 0, hit the stopwatch in the effects panel

3. Move down the timeline 10 key frames

4. Increase the box radius to 60

5. Turn on **Repeat Edge Pixels**

After turning on these settings, your screen should look similar to this:

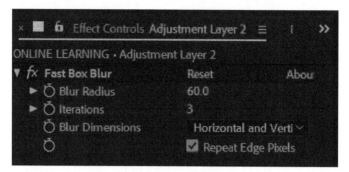

Fast box blur

Great! Let's take a look at what we are working with here. As the fake camera moves in and out on the monitor, all the elements animated on the screen blur as the next message is animating on. I just taught you another transition effect. This is a rack focus transition. You have a lot of tools under your belt so far. Take a breather to be proud of what you have accomplished so far. Next, we are moving on to character animation — my favorite subject.

Character animation types

Character animation is a deep rabbit hole where you can spend years and years learning. Thankfully, you can learn a few simple tricks to get you up and running fast! These tricks will change your life, because character animation will empower you to use characters to express yourself!

Puppet Warp animation

Puppet Warp is one of the most basic character animation tools. You can start using this right now and get immediate results:

1. Import the male puppet

2. Be sure to import the Illustrator file with **Retain layer sizes** and **Create a comp** checked

3. Duplicate this composition and put both in the PRECOMPS folder

4. Move the folders with the Illustrator images into the IMAGES folder

5. Open one of the male puppet precompositions

6. Turn on **Continuous rasterize**

7. Select everything except the torso and parent all the pieces to the torso

8. Copy all the pieces and paste them into the online learning composition

9. Add three pins to the arm, as shown in the following screenshot

Puppet Warp is located up in the tool panel, on the far-right end:

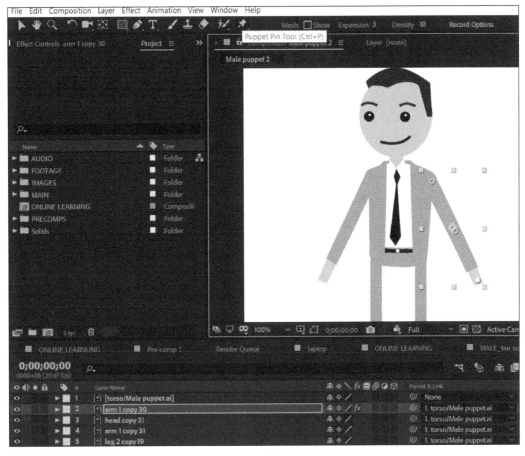

Puppet Warp

In order to animate this, twirl down the **Effects** tab of the arm you added the pins to. Now you can see that key frames have already been added to the layer. Go 30 frames to the right and move the arm to the position, as shown here:

Puppet Warp key frames

As you can see, as you move the pin it creates key frames in the timeline. Preview this to see what we are working with here. Voila! You've got some warpy character animation. If it looks strange, don't worry — you can always tweak it more to your liking. Subtlety is the key to this effect. This effect works best with subtle minor movements.

Jointed animation

This next animation style is called **jointed animation**. It's very versatile and can work well for more realistic movements. You have greater control with jointed animation. With this technique, you need to rig your character just right. Let's duplicate our male puppet composition again and set it up as we did before by turning on continuous rasterized for all layers.

Now that you have created a Puppet Warp animation, we can create a jointed animation. Here's how we can do that:

1. Parent your arms, legs, and head to the torso.

2. Move the arm anchor points to the joints nearest to the torso.

3. Do this for the legs and the head:

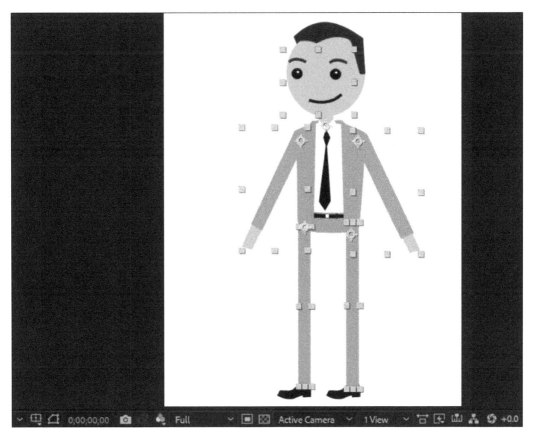

Puppet anchor points

Did you notice how all the anchor points touch the torso? These limbs are rotating around that point.

Follow these instructions to animate your jointed character:

1. Choose an arm and select the **Rotation** parameter

2. Hit a rotation key frame and move down the timeline to the right by 10 key frames

3. Rotate your character arm so it's pointing out to the left

4. Ease those key frames

This is very basic, but imagine all the possibilities! If you had a character with biceps, triceps, thighs, calves, hands, and feet layers, you could parent them correctly and have a fully rigged character that animates! The possibilities are endless.

Adobe Character Animator

Character Animator is by far the most amazing character animation program in After Effects. Install Photoshop and Adobe Character Animator on your machine this very second. With this software, you can create characters that lip synch to your voice. You must have a webcam to create and stream live motion-captured animation online.

First things first, you need to install Adobe Character Animator. When you open Character Animator, you're presented with the **Start** menu. This has free puppets you can start using without editing them. You also have access to interactive tutorials. If you click the right arrow, you can see more free characters to use:

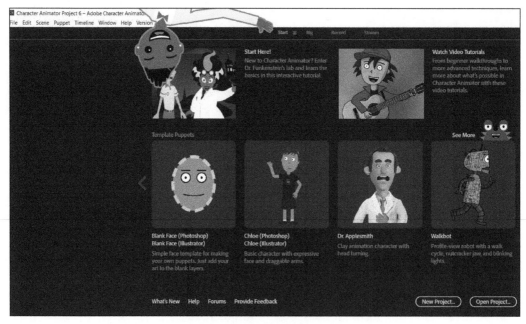

Start menu

Let's click on the **Chloe** character. Choose the Illustator version. You could also use the Photoshop version, but for this lesson we will use the illustrator file. This opens the Chloe character in Illustrator. You can choose to edit the character here, but do not rename anything. Just for fun, let's change the color of her shirt to yellow. Look on the far-left of your Illustrator tool panel and choose the direct selection tool.

Altering Illustrator files

Now that you know how to open your characters, we can start altering our illustrator files. Here's how we do that:

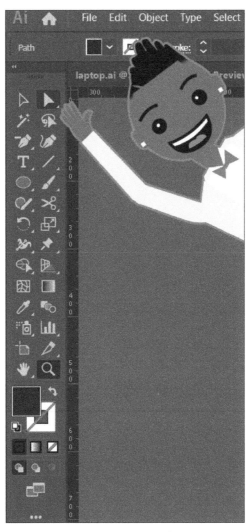

Direct selection tool

Hover the direct selection tool over the different parts of the t-shirt. Click on each piece while holding the *Shift* key:

Select the shirt

Now that the t-shirt is selected, navigate to the left of the tool panel and choose **Fill (X)** to change the color to yellow:

Change color

I am also going to select the t-shirt logo and turn it off. You need to save your Illustrator file, then jump back into Character Animator.

Now you should see the **Record** interface. This is where you animate your character. Let's save this project:

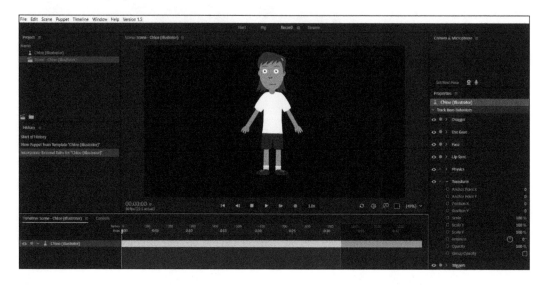

Record interface

Go up to the **File** tab and **Save Project As...**. Give your project a unique name:

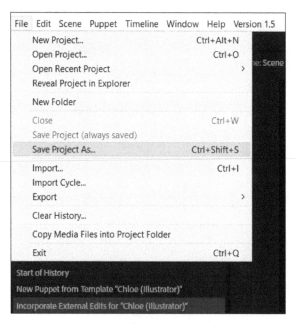

Save as

Character Animator has an autosave feature built into it. I find it useful to save different versions of my projects as I progress. That way, if a project gets corrupted, you will have a backup.

Character Animator interface

The interface is similar to After Effects, except it doesn't have as many tools and panels. To the far left, you will see a **Project** panel window. This is where you can create new scenes and new folders, and organize your project. This is where you import items into the program:

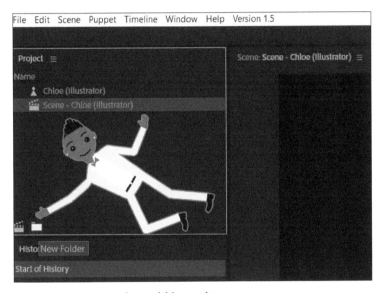

Image folders and new scenes

To the left, at the top of the interface, there are four tabs: **Start/Rig/Record/Stream**. We already looked at the **Start** tab. Let's look at the **Rig** tab. This is where the puppet is rigged. This allows us to take a behind-the-scenes look at our character. As you get more advanced, you will need to edit the rig of your character here:

Rig

The **Record** tab is the animation panel; this is where all the animation and performance takes place.

The **Stream** tab is used for streaming your performance live around the world:

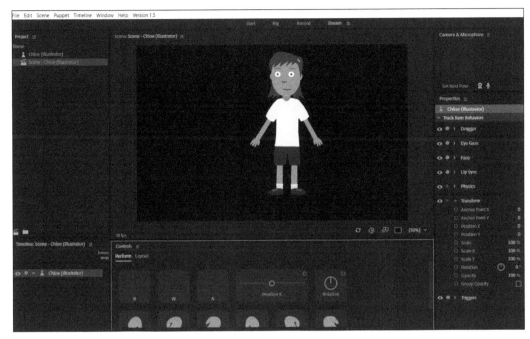

Stream

Next, let's look at the scene **Properties**.

Make sure your scene is selected, then look to the far-right—you will see a variety of project settings you can adjust, such as **Frame Rate**:

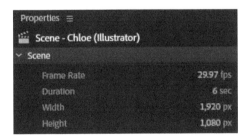

Scene settings

The **Scene** window is where your character is. This is where all the action takes place. Take a look at the play buttons under the character. This allows you to go backward or forward in the timeline. The red button is how you record your animations. To the right of the Record button is the speed. You can control how quickly or slowly your recording happens:

Record button and speed

Next, let's look at the camera and mic panel.

This is where you handle your webcam setup and your voice recording. Let's turn on our webcam. Click this camera input tab at the top-left corner of the interface. If you have a working webcam, you should see the box in the panel show your image in it. This will enable facial tracking. The red dots are track points on your face:

Image webcam

Let's make sure our face is properly synced. Make sure you have a strong light source. Also, wearing glasses can interfere with syncing your face to the web camera. Next, select the webcam button. Click the (**Set Rest Pose**). This will sync your face to the character's face. It's similar to what happened in Avatar when Sully gets synced to his avatar. Now you are synced to your character:

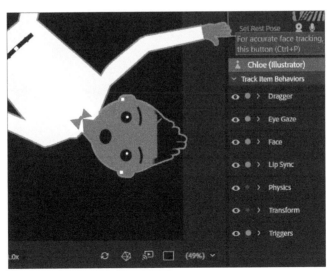

Set Rest Pose

Now you can spend some time playing with your character—when you speak, it speaks. It only syncs to your head; as its head will move with yours, its eyes will also follow yours. It will also speak when you speak. I'll show you how to move its limbs later.

Animation timeline

Let's look at the **animation timeline**. This is where you can see your layers and is similar to After Effects. You can edit your performances here:

Timeline

Next, we will look at the character properties. Select your **Chloe** character layer in the timeline. To the far right, you have properties for her eyes, face, lips, and so on:

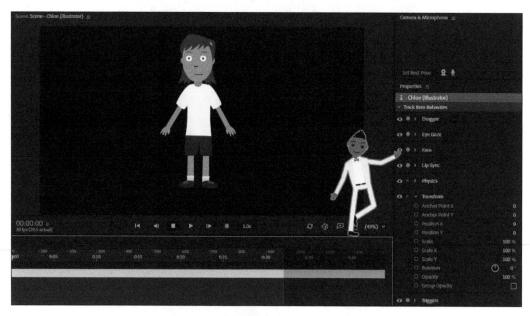

Puppet properties

Recording your performance

These are all the properties you can adjust for your character.

Now that we know where everything is located, let's begin our animation and our performance:

1. Click on the red record button. You will hear a few beeps before the recording button is active:

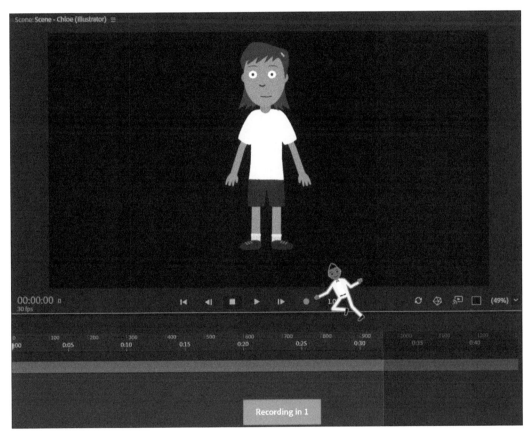

Record button

2. Select Chloe's hand and drag it.
3. Let go of her hand.
4. Press the record button again to stop recording.

Adjusting character properties

It may take your computer a couple of seconds to render the recording. When it's done, you will have a recording layer. This is called a **take** in Character Animator. You can adjust your **Dragger** setting like this:

1. Select the character in the timeline and to the right in the **Properties**.

2. Twirl down the **Dragger** properties:

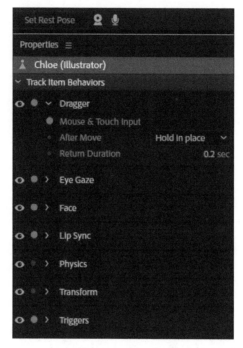

Dragger properties

Across from the **After Move** property, you can choose to hold your limbs in place or return to rest. Let's choose **Return to rest**. This will enable our limbs to return to their original resting pose after moving them:

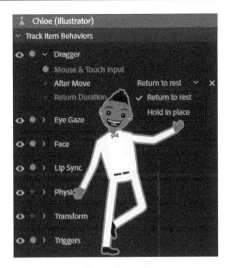

Return to rest

You can also adjust **Eye Gaze** to control the strength or the extent to which the eyes will move:

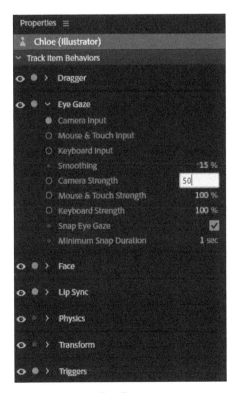

Eye Gaze

Let's look at our **Face** controls. These are located on the far-right of your screen. We won't go over all these parameters here, but you can change your **Eyebrow Strength** to 40. This will give you control of eyebrow movements. If you need to adjust anything on the face, this is where you find it:

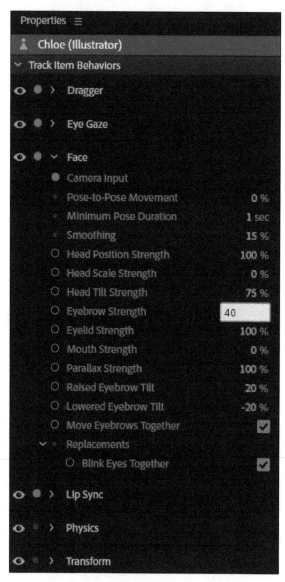

Face controls

We are almost ready to start the animation. Look in the far-right corner of the screen—there is a small camera-control icon. Click on this icon to begin to activate your camera. Hit the record button to activate live recording:

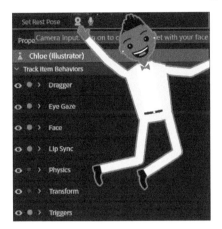

Camera control

If you move your head around, you should see your puppet moving. Let's adjust the gravity for her hair:

Gravity Strength

You will need to zoom into the timeline to look at the bottom corner of the panel, just under the timeline. You will see an icon similar to that in After Effects. Click on this to zoom into the timeline:

Zoom into the timeline

Blending takes

After you're done with your performance, press the record button again. You will see the recordings on your timeline. You can edit these by sliding them, or you may want to blend or ease your performances. This is similar to easing a movement in After Effects. These layers are called **takes** and are similar to an acting performance in a movie. An actor has a series of **takes** in a movie scene:

1. Select the end of your take layer.
2. You will see a double-arrow icon.
3. Drag this icon to the left. You will see a sloped curve icon. This means you can blend or smooth the end of your take layer:

Blend take

Starting recording

Next, let's make Chloe talk! Look at the icon next to the camera. This is the audio recording button:

1. Click on the audio button.
2. Click the record button.
3. Begin speaking.

4. Click the record button again to stop recording:

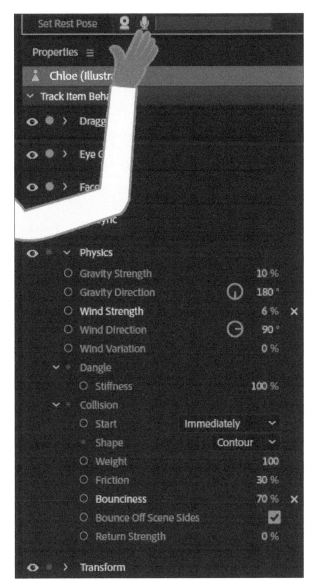

Turn on the audio button

This will add additional **Audio** layers in the timeline. Take a look at the new layers or takes in the timeline here:

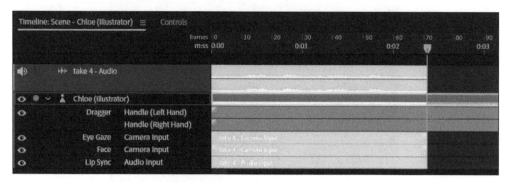

Camera and audio input layers

Now that we've created a cool animation, let's play it to preview our work. Press the play button:

Play button

Project settings

Now that you know how to animate your character and record audio, let's adjust our project settings. The following steps will show you how to do that:

1. Select the **Scene**.

2. Look at the far-right and you will see the **Scene** info.

3. Adjust the scene **Duration** so that it's only the length of your project:

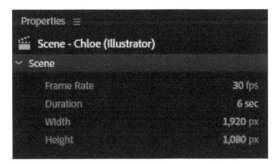

Adjust scene duration

Next, we are going to adjust our **Frame Rate** so that it matches our frame rate in After Effects. Change this to 29.97 fps:

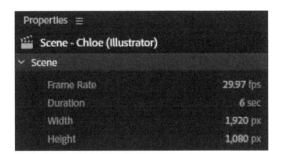

Adjust scene duration frame rate

Exporting your animation

Now let's export our project. Your project will export with a transparent background unless you put an image in the background.

The following are the steps to export your project:

1. Click on **File**.

2. Click on **Export**.

3. Select **PNG Sequence and WAV...**:

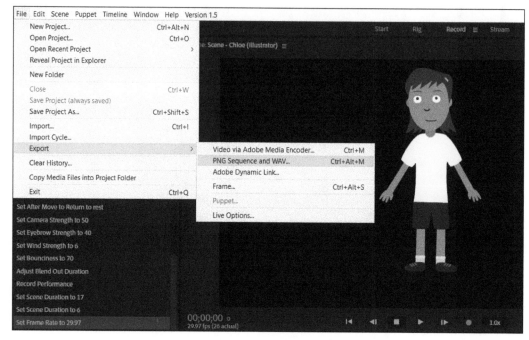

Export PNG sequence

Importing PNG sequences

We are ready to import our PNG sequences. Here are the steps to do that:

1. Jump back over to After Effects. Import the .png file.

2. Select the first .png file with 00 at the end.

3. After Effects will import all the remaining files in a .png sequence.

4. Ensure that you check the sequence:

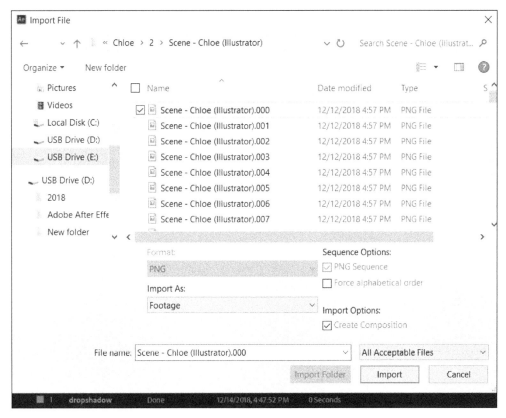

Import PNG

You can also import any audio recorded in your character animation. When you render out your PNG sequence, it will save a WAV file with it. If you need to import your audio file, here are the steps:

1. Go to the folder with the PNG sequence.
2. Navigate to the bottom of the PNG sequence.

3. Import the WAV file to After Effects:

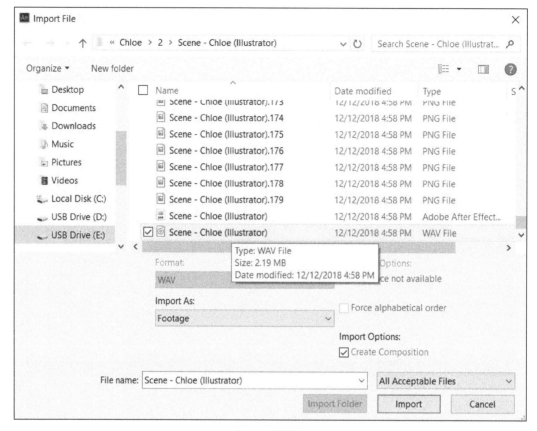

Import WAV

Adding the character to an infographic project

Now we are going to bring Chloe into the main composition and we are going to create a camera move to the right. We will animate our null object to do this. We need to be on the correct part of the timeline and we need the correct things parented to the null.

To be sure we are at the correct point on the timeline, follow these steps:

1. Move to the point on the timeline after the last bit of text that has been animated on.

2. Move the Chloe layer on to the timeline so that the layer starts at that point.

3. Turn on motion blur for Chloe. See the placement of everything here:

Camera pan start point

We need to parent the Chloe layer to the null layer at this point. Also parent the text to the null layer:

Parent character to null

To create a hold key frame for the position parameter of our null object, follow these steps:

1. Navigate to the far-right of the timeline.

2. Locate the diamond icon in the position of the null object.

3. Click on the diamond:

Blank key frame

Let's animate our move to the right. Select the position parameter and scrub it so that the camera is moving to the right:

Pan to Chloe

Completing your infographic

You now have all the tools to create a dynamic infographic video. Spend some time adding more text to help communicate your concept.

Summary

In this chapter, we have learned how to create infographics. These types of videos can be used to communicate information, explain products, or as a way to express stories. You have learned many skills and tools. You can create kinetic typography and edit it. You can also animate icons in dynamic, realistic ways, as demonstrated with this project. The biggest thing you learned was how to animate characters. You learned three different ways to bring characters to life. Experiment with these character animation tools.

I have provided additional links for further reading. Character animation is a valuable skill to have in your toolbox. It allows you to add humor and emotion to your projects, and is a unique way to engage your viewers! We also covered different camera moves such as a camera push in and a left-to-right pan. These camera moves are a great way to transition in and out of scenes. We also covered using adjustment layers to simulate a rack focus. You now have a variety of character animation tools at your disposal. I strongly recommend you experiment with all of these character animation tools. Use these characters to help tell your story!

In the next chapter, we will create a film title. This will build on your knowledge of text animation and effects.

Questions

1. What is tracking used for?
2. What should Illustrator files should be imported as?
3. Why is it important to turn on continuously rasterize for Illustrator layers?
4. Why is it important to turn on Easy Ease for your key frames?
5. In Adobe Character Animator, how do you turn on facial tracking and lip-synch recording?
6. How do you export your Adobe Character Animator project?
7. How many locations does motion blur need to be turned on at?

Further reading

Adobe Character Animator is a deep program. Take some time to read more about animation principles and this amazing program, and what you can do with it:

- `https://www.adobe.com/products/character-animator.html`
- `https://www.creativebloq.com/advice/understand-the-12-principles-of-animation`

5
Producing a Film Title Project Using Text Animator

In this chapter, we will learn how to create a film title. Film titles are shown at the beginning of a movie. These short sequences not only provide the name of the movie, but also set the tone for the film. Contemporary film titles were created by Saul Bass. His films, such as **Psycho** and the **Man with the Golden Arm**, revolutionized film titles. He elevated film titles to an art form.

In this chapter, we will learn the following:

- How to create a mood with exciting type!
- Special 3D effects for our type to give it depth
- How to use trackmates to add texture

Creating a film title

Imagine this: you are in a movie theater and the film starts; then you see a dramatic title on the screen. This title not only provides the name of the film, but it puts you in the mood for the movie you're about to watch. Any seasoned After Effects artist knows how to create film titles. In this chapter, we will build on our tools and skills from previous lessons, such as type design. But we will also dive into new skills, such as using more effects and using After Effects lights. Let's get started!

Setting up your project

The first thing we're going to do is create a 1,920 x 1,080 comp in After Effects. Let's set this up by going through the following steps:

1. Make this comp five seconds long.

2. Name it NIGHT KINGDOM (or the name of your film title).

3. Make it 29.97.

4. Create five folders. Name them Precomp, Main, and Images.

Now that you have your project set up, we are going to add a solid background to our composition. Make this background solid black, by selecting the option shown in the following screenshot. This background will be at the bottom of our layers:

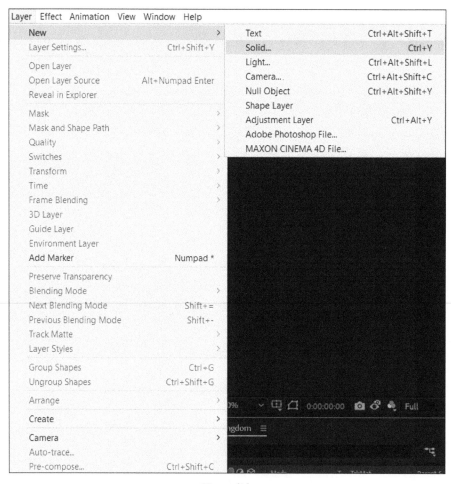

New solid

Now we are going to create a text layer by selecting the option shown in the following screenshot:

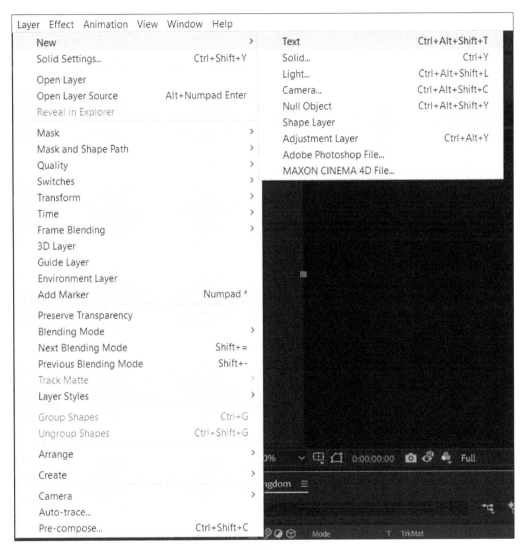

Text layer

When you add a text layer, it will come into your composition centered, but completely blank. It's up to you to add text to it. You can do this by going through the following steps:

1. Type NIGHT on the first line
2. Type KINGDOM on the second line
3. Change your font to Constantia or to any sans serif font
4. Parent the KINGDOM line of type with the NIGHT line of type

When creating titles, you will need to make sure your text is lined up and conforms to title-safe guidelines. Take a look at where these guidelines are located. Turn on the **Title/Action Safe** option, as shown in the following screenshot. Familiarize yourself with these guides and add them to your arsenal of tools when creating any type in After Effects:

Title safe

Adjust the scale of the NIGHT type so the entire title fits into the title-safe guideline, as shown in the following screenshot:

We are going for a stylized fantasy look for our title sequence. To achieve this, we will scale up the first letter of each line by going through the following steps:

1. Select your text tool.
2. Select the first letter of each line of type.
3. Go over to the text-sizing parameter in the upper-left corner of the character panel.

4. Drag the sizing parameter up so your first letter is scaled up, as shown in the following screenshot:

Scale text

Repeat this process for the K in KINGDOM.

Creating 3D-looking text with bevel emboss

We want to further stylize this text by creating a 3D-looking effect for the title. Let's use the bevel emboss layer style. Layer styles are a great way to add additional features to your layers. To begin with, we need to precompose both of our type layers and then name this precomp type. Go through the following steps to add a bevel emboss style to your text:

1. Go to your text precomp.

2. Select the NIGHT text layer.

3. Go to **Layer** and navigate to **Layer Styles**.

4. Click on **Bevel and Emboss** to apply this to your text, as shown in the following screenshot:

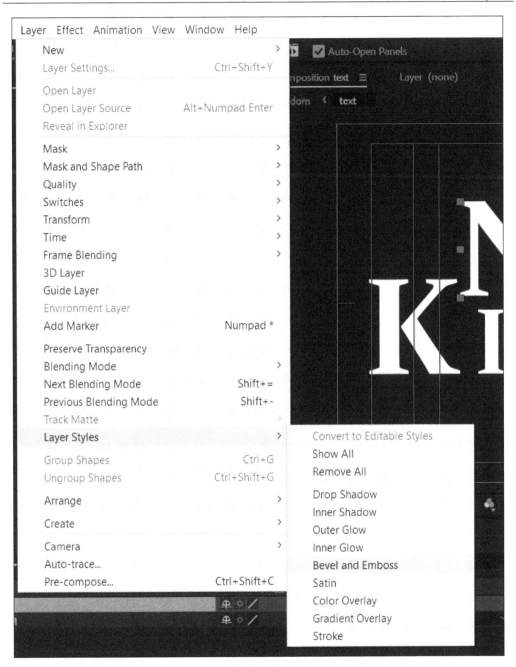

Bevel emboss

Next, we are going to tweak our bevel settings. To adjust the settings, simply scroll down our text settings and reveal the layer styles. Look at the settings in the following screenshot and adjust your settings as I have. The main change to make is to switching your technique to **Chisel Hard**, as shown in the following screenshot:

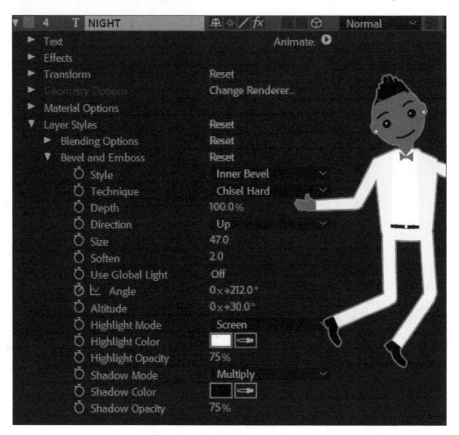

Bevel emboss settings

Now that you have your emboss settings configured, you can copy your layer style and paste it on to you KINGDOM text, as shown in the following screenshot:

Layer style paste

We want to give our text more dramatic lighting, so we are going to add an effect called **CC Glass** by going through the following steps:

1. Go back to your main title comp.
2. Go to the **Effects** panel.

3. Add the effect called **CC Glass** to your text precomp, as shown in the following screenshot:

CC Glass

You may notice that you get a bit of shiny lighting effect to your type. Let's go on a little adventure and explore the settings for **CC Glass**. This effect is used to give things a shiny glass-like look. However, we are going to use it to give our text light effects. The first setting to adjust is the light settings. We want to add a light to our scene by going through the following steps:

1. Go to **Layer**.

2. Navigate through the **New** tab.

3. Choose **Light...**, as shown in the following screenshot:

Add light

Take a look at these **Light Settings**. We are creating a point light with the color white. Ensure that you check **Casts Shadows**, as shown in the following screenshot:

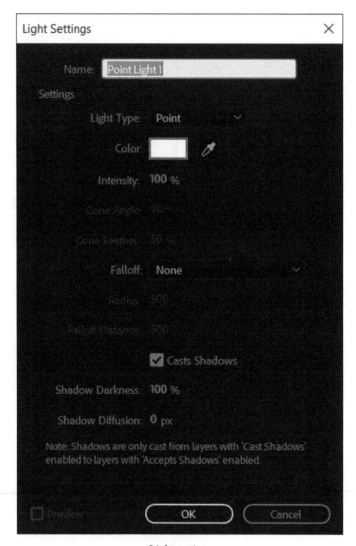

Light setting

We will go into lights in much more detail in future lessons. For now, it's enough to know that this light mimic is an actual light in your composition. Objects will respond as if it's an actual light. Let's make some adjustments to our light by going through the following steps:

1. Create a null object
2. Parent your light with it

This will allow you to move your light easily. When you want to move your light, simply move the null object by going through the following steps:

1. Select your text precomp.

2. Go to the **CC Glass** parameters.

3. Scroll down the **Light** settings.

4. Choose **Using | AE Lights**, as shown in the following steps:

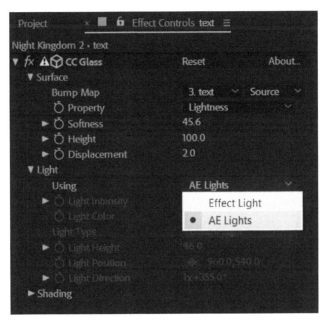

CC Glass settings

Move your null object around. You should see that the light follows it. You're there — real light glints on your text! How awesome is this? You are ready to rock and roll with **CC Glass** settings to further improve your sexy text! I am going to leave the tweaking of these settings up to you; I set my softness at 45 percent — this soothes out the glass effect. You can copy my settings if you want; they are all in the preceding screenshot.

Take a few moments here to adjust your **Light** settings. I'll provide you an image with my settings, but you can adjust yours more or less as you see fit. You can find your **Light** settings by scrolling down the light layer and selecting the **Light Options** setting, as shown in the following screenshot:

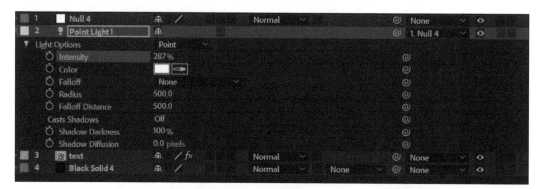

Light setting

As you can see, I increased the intensity to 287. We may change this later, but as you can see, this is how you increase the light amount.

Next, we are going to tweak our glass setting further and add a level effect. The levels are found in the effects. Double-click on this to add this effect to your text precomp. We will tweak these setting to get a sharper contrast for our text, as shown in the following screenshot:

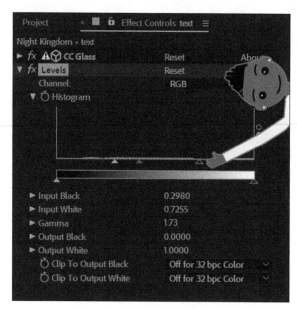

Levels

Adjust your **Levels** settings (the histogram) so that you can crush your blacks and whites. This will give your text more contrast. Let's set this up by going through the following steps:

1. Change your **CC Glass** height setting to 40
2. Change your **CC Glass** softness to 25

Let's take a moment and take stock of what we have so far. We have some 3D text that's lit well with a light. Next, we need to give it more drama and atmosphere. We are going to animate our light and add some atmospheric smoke to the scene. This is a fantasy movie, so we want our environment to look and feel mysterious and otherworldly.

Light animation

Let's animate our light in this scene by animating the null object that the light is parented with. We can set this up by going through the following steps:

1. Select your null object.
2. Press P for **Position**.
3. Start at the beginning of the timeline and animate to the **2** second mark in the timeline, as shown in the following screenshot.
4. Animate your light so that it moves from left to right over your text:

Light animation

Next, let's scroll down our light options to reveal the **Color** options for our light. Change the **Color** of your light to a light blue, as shown in the following screenshot:

Color adjustment

Using track mattes

This is looking good so far. Let's improve our titles by giving them some texture. Choose the **Grunge** texture. We will use this as the texture for our type.

Go into your text precomp and select both lines of text, as shown in the following screenshot:

Text selection

Next, precompose these text layers. We can now put a texture on both of these at the same time. Find the **Grunge** layer and bring the **Grunge** image into the text layer with the precomped text. Put the **Grunge** layer under the text layer, as shown in the following screenshot:

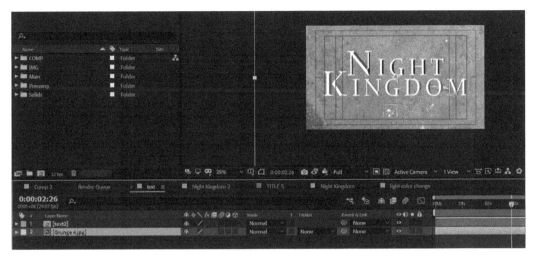

Grunge layer 1

Nice! Now we can add a track matte to our texture. Track mattes allow you to use a layer or mask as a matte. The program will use the text as a stencil for the texture.

Choose the texture and select the **Alpha** track matte by going through the following steps:

1. Select your Grunge layer.
2. Look the right-hand side of the **Track Matte** tab.
3. Scroll down the **Track Matte** tab.

4. Choose the **Alpha Matte "[text2]"**, as shown in the following screenshot:

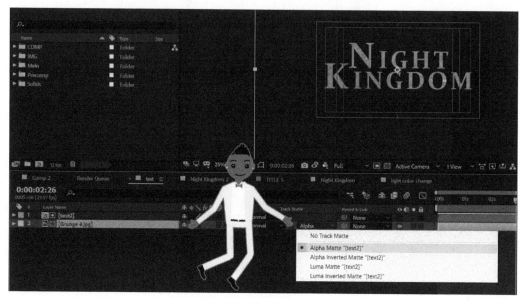

Alpha track matte

Track matte is a fierce tool. You can fill anything with the texture of your choice. This empowers you to use a variety of images and create interesting realistic objects. I encourage you to dive deep into using track mattes. Experiment and have fun with all the possibilities.

But there's a problem: we've lost our 3D effect. When you add a track matte to a layer, it will fill your layer with that image, flattening your text. Here's a simple solution:

1. Duplicate your text layer.

2. Make sure it's turned on.

3. To the right, you will find the blend modes.

4. Select **Overlay**, as shown in the following screenshot:

Overlay blend modes

Blend modes is a helpful set of tools to have to hand. Blend modes are like Photoshop modes, where you can determine how the layers blend with each other. Now that you have the overlay blend mode on, you can see that the text layer is overlaying its visual properties on top of the Grunge layer.

If you're at all like me, you like to tweak your settings until they are perfect. Let's tweak our levels to ensure that most of the texture is coming through on our text, as shown in the following screenshot:

Level adjustment

This is looking good! Let's add some atmosphere to our title by going through the following steps:

1. Add an adjustment layer
2. Add a **Fog lights** effects to the adjustment layer
3. Name your adjustment layer **Fog light**

This is a great effect that will work for you without further adjustments. It will give you a fog-like background with animation. If you look at the fog-light layer, you will notice that this effect comes with its own keyframes. You're free to move these keyframes to make the fog move faster or slower, as shown in the following screenshot:

Fog lights effect

Let's add some additional color to our background by going through the following steps:

1. Select the **Fog lights** layer.
2. Add the **Hue/Saturation** effect.
3. Check the **Color** option in the **Hue/Saturation** effect panel.
4. Adjust the hue until the color turns blue.

5. Adjust the lightness to make the background a bit darker, as shown in the following screenshot:

Hue/Saturation

Lens flares

As we head our discussion to **Lens Flares**, it is imperative to know that it is an art form of its own. Through this feature you can create unique effects that is bound to evoke the drama your project needs. Let's create a custom lens flare effect by going through the following steps:

1. We are going to create a new comp for a lens flare.
2. Create a new composition that is 500 x 500.

3. Name this `flare`, as shown in the following screenshot:

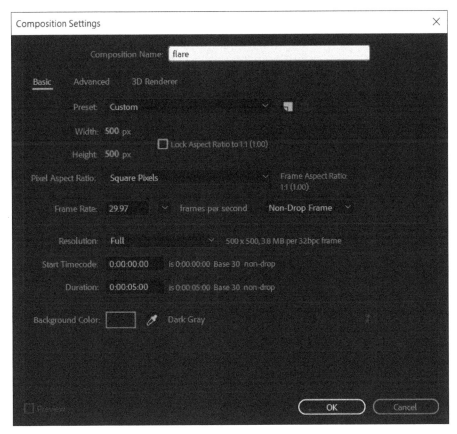

New comp

4. Create an adjustment.
5. Create a new black solid.

6. Add a lens flare effect to the adjustment, as shown in the following screenshot:

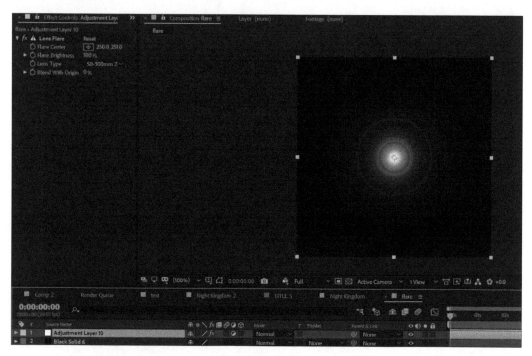

Flare

7. Next, let's mask our flare.

8. Select the ellipse mask tool and mask around our flare.

9. Mask your flare.

10. Feather out your mask, as shown in the following screenshot:

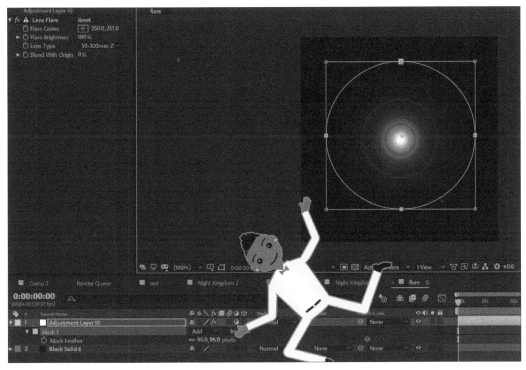

Mask and feather

11. Now bring this flare precomp into our title composition.

12. Switch the blending mode to **Add**.

13. Add the **Hue/Saturation** effect.

14. Check the color box.

15. Adjust the color to yellow.

16. Scale this flare down, as shown in the following screenshot:

Hue/Saturation

You're doing great work here. Let's animate the opacity of the light on. Make sure your flare doesn't have a square border; feather your mask in the precomp to achieve this. The final step is to render the title. This is a five-second movie, so make your composition for this project render only five seconds in length.

Summary

Title design is an essential skill set that you need as a motion designer. For this project, we put into practice the lessons that we previously learned about type design, and we learned about 3D bevel effects. We also learned how to work with texture using track mattes. You should master this and keep practicing with track mattes. This will help you tremendously in your growth as a motion graphic animator. We also learned how to create a lens flare effect and we started working with lights.

In the next chapter, we will work with sports graphics. We will use more text-related skills, learn about motion tracking, and much more.

Questions

1. What is a track matte?

2. How do you add a light?

3. What is a bevel effect?

4. What is a hue/saturate effect?

5. What is a lens flare?

6. What are levels?

7. What does title-safe mean?

Further reading

Check out these revolutionary film titles by Saul Bass:

- `https://www.imdb.com/title/tt0048347/`

- `https://www.imdb.com/title/tt0054215/`

- `http://www.artofthetitle.com/designer/saul-bass/`

Section 2: Video, Visual Effects, Compositing

In this section, you will discover and work with basic and advanced special effects to sharpen your skills.

The following chapters are included in this section:

- *Chapter 6, Animating Sports Graphics with Compositing Effects*
- *Chapter 7, Develop a VFX Project Using the 3D Camera Tracker*

6

Animating Sports Graphics with Compositing Effects

Sport motion graphics capture the power and excitement of competitive sports. They are filled with energy and get your heart pumping. In this chapter, we are going to create a sports graphics package utilizing dynamic logos and effects. We will also master compositing by combining video footage and images in a convincing way in our project. Knowing how to composite scenes and create realistic graphics from random video and image sources is critical as a motion graphic artist. We will use the powerful camera tracking effects in this chapter. Camera tracking is a way to track video layers and then use that data to composite text, logos, videos, and images in your scene.

We will use lens flare and other effects as transition elements in our project. By the end of this chapter, you will have a clear understanding of compositing, tracking, and effects to create dynamic realistic projects.

The following topics will be covered in this chapter:

- Compositing
- Camera tracking
- Creative transitions
- Color correcting videos

Creating sports motion graphics

Sports graphics are dynamic, exciting, and very often informative. They are perfect for motion graphics. We will learn how to create custom lens flares and how to use tracking to create realistic compositions.

Setting up your project

Our first scene will involve an animated logo. We will introduce a football team's logo in a dramatic and entertaining way. You can either use your own logo, or you can use the logo design provided in the *Technical requirements* section of this chapter. So, let's begin the setup by completing the following tasks:

1. Create a comp with dimensions of 1920 x 1080. Name it `Sports Graphic`.
2. Create a solid shape for our background and name this `background`.
3. Select the background layer and add a fill effect to it.
4. Use the fill effect to change the background layer to a deep blue-black color.
5. Change the resolution to a quarter.

Now that we are all set, let's create an environment for our sports animation project.

Creating an environment

An environment can be an indoor or outdoor setting for a scene. A good environment can help to bring life to the entire scene. Let's create one for our sports logo. We'll create an effect that depicts a floor in our environment. The floor in our environment will provide a surface against which we will add a nice reflection of our logo. Use the following screenshot as a reference, and follow these steps:

1. Create a black solid layer.
2. Name the layer `floor blur`.
3. Move this layer to the top of the timeline.
4. Mask a narrow rectangle shape for the lower section of the floor.
5. Feather the mask to 160 so that the edges are blurred:

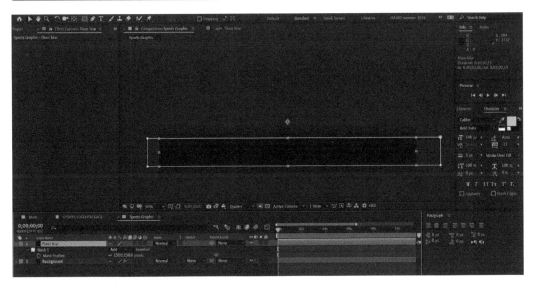

An environment

This is the first step toward creating a floor for our environment. Next, we will add some light for our flash effect.

Using custom light effects

Although After Effects comes with a lens flare effect, we are going to create some custom light effects for our projects. The ability to create your own light effects will be a great asset to have in your toolkit for creating dynamic motion graphics.

Let's create a custom light effect for our project:

1. Create a comp with dimensions of 400 x 400.

2. Name it `Light 1`.

3. Add a **Solid** layer to this comp.

4. Add a **Lens Flare** effect and make it small.

5. Center this flare.

6. Add the **Hue/Saturation** effect.

7. Choose **Colorize**. Make the color light blue.

8. Add a **Fast Blur (Legacy)** effect to this layer.

9. Draw a circle mask around the flare and then feather this mask:

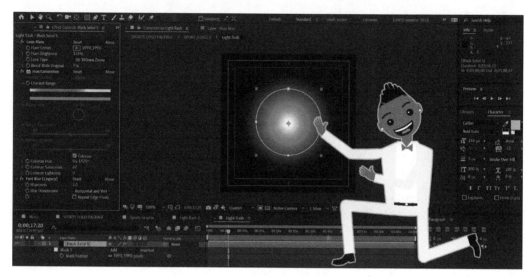

A custom light effect

When you're finished with the preceding steps, your light should look like the previous screenshot. Next, we are going to composite and animate our lights in the main project.

Animating flashing lights

Now, we're going to bring our light into our sports graphics main comp and animate these lights coming on. These lights should animate on and off quickly, like a physical light flashing on and off. The following steps will demonstrate how to do this.

These lights need to be composited into our scene. The steps for animating the lights are similar to our previous projects:

1. Bring the light comp into the Sports Graphic comp.

2. Turn on the **Add** mode for the light comp.

3. Animate the properties of **Rotation**, **Opacity**, and **Scale** for five key frames.

4. Easy ease all key frames:

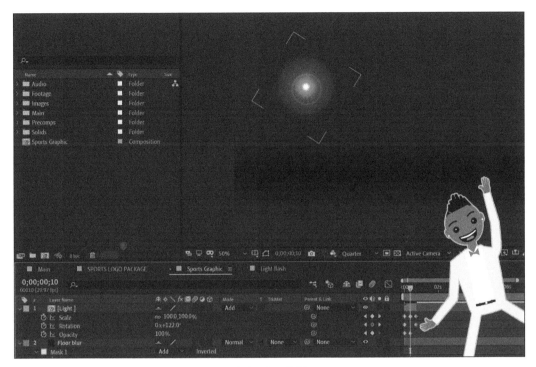

Animating light

5. Trim your **Light** precomp.
6. Duplicate the precomp with all the animation key frames you created.

7. Have the lights flash on and off at different times throughout the entire five second introduction sequence:

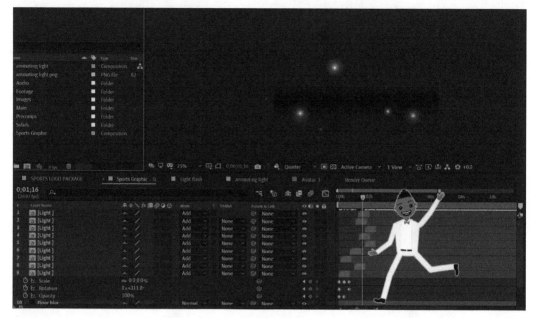

Duplicating lights

Now, you can spread the lights across the timeline, as demonstrated in the preceding screenshot. In the next section, we will animate the sports logo.

Animating your sports logo

The sports logo needs to move substantially and exude a lot of energy. Imagine that you're watching a game. You are anxiously waiting for your team to play. When you finally see the team's logo, you feel excited. You want your logo animation to convey this energy to the viewer.

The overall goal of the following steps is to animate the logo on the screen in a dynamic way. The logo will animate on the screen quickly in the beginning, and slow down at the end:

1. Import your logo.

2. Bring the logo into the sports graphics comp.

3. To the right of the layer, you will find a continuously rasterized button. Turn this on.

4. Scale up your logo so that it takes up the entire screen. Hit the **Scale** stopwatch to create a key frame.

5. Add the **Fast Box Blur** effect.

6. Hit the stopwatch for blur radius.

7. Turn the radius up to 80.

8. Check repeat edges.

9. Make the logo blurry in the first frame of the intro:

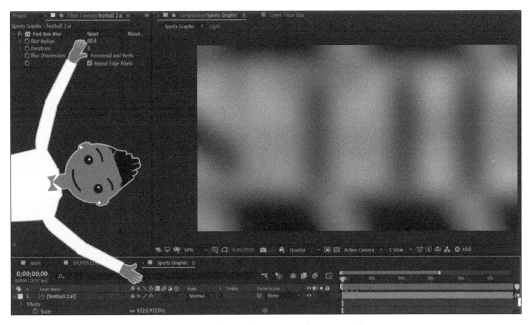

Fast box blur and continuously rasterized

The next step is to animate the logo back down to a normal size. We also need to animate the blur effect back to zero. We want the logo to have an effect of slamming into the scene aggressively.

Follow these steps to further composite and animate the effects for your logo:

1. Add a glow effect. Key frame the radius stopwatch at 0.

2. Move down five key frames.

3. Set the key frame radius stopwatch to 140.

4. Move down five key frames and reduce the radius to 0.

5. Move back to the beginning of the comp.

6. Move down the timeline to 30 key frames.

7. Reduce the scale parameter of the logo.

8. Position the logo on the black background line.

9. Reduce the blur to 0.

10. Turn on motion blur for the logo.

Great job! These steps will help our logo look like it's in a real environment by using the glow and blur effects. The exciting thing is that these are completely editable, and you can adjust your effects until they feel realistic. Let's continue cruising with our project by creating a logo reflection effect.

Adding a reflection

We need to add believable elements to what we are trying to composite. In this case, it's our logo. We want the logo to look like it belongs in the scene. We will accomplish that by creating a reflection to our scene.

Let's create our reflection with these steps:

1. Duplicate and rename the logo to `Reflect logo`.

2. To reflect your logo layer, go to **Transform** and choose **Flip vertical**.

3. Delete all key frames on the **Logo** layer.

4. Go to the last key frame for the **Logo** scale.

5. Position `Reflect logo` so that it touches the bottom of the logo.

6. Parent `Reflect logo` to **Logo**.

7. Add a **Fast Box Blur** effect to reflect the logo layer at a radius of `5`.

8. Turn down the `Reflect logo` opacity to `10`.

9. Easy ease **Logo** scale key frames:

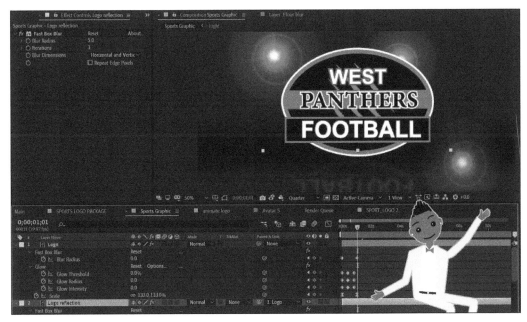

Eased key frames

As you can see, the scale key frames are easy eased. This will give the key frames a smooth movement.

Creating camera movement

Camera movements are crucial to catch the viewer's eye. You want your scene to always have some movement in it. This is really important in motion graphics, as we need to keep the viewer entertained.

We are going to create continuous, subtle camera movements. Follow these steps:

1. Parent the logo to a **Null** object.
2. Go to 4 seconds in the comp.
3. Select the **Null** object.
4. Add a key frame to the scale parameter.
5. Go to the beginning of the comp.

6. Increase the scale of the **Null** object to 150.

7. Add easy ease to the **Null** object key frames

8. Duplicate and reposition the light comp throughout the four seconds so that the lights are flashing the entire time.

I hope that you enjoyed creating this null camera move. Any seasoned After Effects artist knows how to employ this technique for quick camera movement. In the next section, we will create a light glint for our project. By the end of this project, you will be a pro at creating and animating light shapes.

Creating another light shape

Let's add other visual interests to our logo animation by creating a new light shape. We'll call this comp Light Glint. We'll create this light by reusing our first one, but we will add more details to it.

A variety of lighting effects will help to add visual interest to our shot. The steps are similar to our previous custom light:

1. Duplicate the Light comp.

2. Rename it Light Glint.

3. Adjust the **Hue/Saturation** to an almost white colorized hue. Add **Solid**.

4. Mask off **Solid** in the shape of a pointed dash.

5. Feather this mask.

6. Turn on the add blend mode.

7. Duplicate the masked shape.

8. Adjust these masks, as shown in the following screenshot.

9. Bring this **Light Glint** animation into the **Sports Graphic** comp.

10. Turn on the add blend mode:

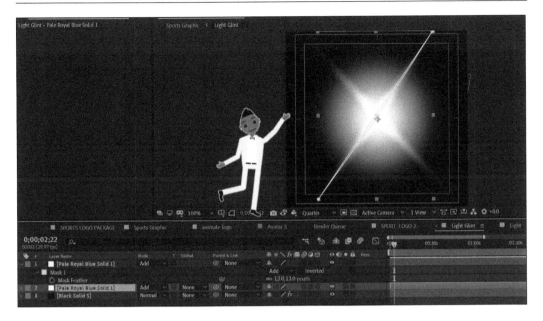

A light glint

Be sure to composite your light effect with the add blend mode. We will animate this light in the next section.

Animating the light glint

Now that we have a new light, let's animate this along the rim of the logo. We will animate this just as the logo settles into its position.

Take your time with these steps, to create a realistic light effect:

1. Position the **Light Glint** animation on the rim of the logo.
2. Scale the light down so that it looks like a small accent.
3. Parent this **Light Glint** animation to the logo layer.
4. Animate the **Opacity** and **Position** of this glint on the edge of the logo.
5. Adjust the motion path with the vertex tool (located next to the pen tool).

6.   The light should fade out and travel along the logo:

The motion path

Add a vignette to the comp

Now that our animation is complete, we need to add a subtle vignette to our composition. This will help composite our scene and create a dramatic lighting effect for our video.

A vignette will help everything look like it belongs in the same scene. You're basically masking a shape and feathering it:

1.   Add a black solid.

2.   Name it Vignette.

3.   Add a large circular mask in the center of the mask.

4.   Under the mask options, choose Subtract.

5.   Add a 200 pixel feather to the mask.

6.   Reduce the vignette opacity to 50%:

Vignette

Now, your scene should look nice and cohesive!

Camera tracking a video

Camera tracking is a process that involves taking a video and tracking its motion, so that 3D elements can be added to it. This process is used in movies and TV shows to add special effects and 3D elements. It's important to know how to track footage in After Effects. Understanding this tool allows you to create realistic visual effects.

Using the following steps, we are going to attach our sports logo to a video of a fence. The goal of this shot is to make the logo look like it belongs in the scene:

1. Import a video into After Effects.
2. Select a video in the project window.
3. Right-click on the video and choose New Comp from Selection.
4. Rename the comp to `Camera Track`.
5. Go into this comp.
6. Trim the video to around `40` frames.

It's important to trim your video so that you're not tracking unnecessary frames. After adding this effect, if you can't see your track points, follow these steps:

1. Twirl open the effect layer.

2. Select the 3D camera tracker to see your track points.

3. To see your targets, you need to hover over the points created by the camera tracker.

4. In order to see the targets, you may need to increase the target size in the camera tracker:

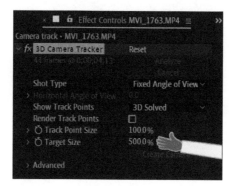

Target size

5. Go to the beginning of the composition.

6. Under effects, type in 3d camera tracker.

7. While the video layer is selected, double-click on effect to add it.

8. Wait while the footage is analyzed.

9. Look under the camera effect. You may need to turn up the Target Size. I turned mine up to 500.

10. Find a good forward-facing target, and right-click.

11. Select **Create Solid and Camera**:

Create solid and camera

This will create a 3D camera in your composition. It will also create a solid for that 3D space. We will go over more 3D tools in future lessons. For this project, we want to replace our solid with our sports logo. We will have to bring our logo into this composition and parent it to the track solid. In order for this logo to be 3D, we have to turn on the 3D cube button. The 3D button is indicated in the following screenshot:

3D button

When you make a layer into a 3D layer, the layer itself remains flat, but it gains an additional property that allows the layer to move in 3D space. Notice the colored arrows.

Compositing a logo in tracked footage

It may look like your logo has disappeared. Do not fear! Just scale your logo up to a ridiculous amount so that you can see it. Now that this layer is 3D, you can move it in the third dimension. You may need to adjust the rotation of the logo so that it's in the same perspective as the fence:

Adjust logo rotation

Now that your logo is properly adjusted, you can turn off the solid layer. Let's create a preview so that we can see how all our hard work has paid off!

Bringing it all together

We have spent a lot of time creating both of our scenes, so now we need to combine them in one dynamic edit! After Effects can be used to edit shots together, and for creative transitions between scenes. Let's composite all our scenes together and add some final touches. These elements will make our scene composite together convincingly. Follow these steps:

1. Copy `Vignette` from the `Sports Graphic` comp.

2. Paste it into the `Camera track` comp.

3. Add an adjustment layer.

4. Add the auto levels effect to the adjustment layer. Adjust this to taste.

5. Add a **Solid** layer.

6. Add the **Lens Flare** effect to the black solid.

7. Turn on the add blending mode.

After you've added the lens flare, you need to adjust the flare center point. Find where the light source is and adjust the center, as indicated in the following screenshot:

Adjusting lens flare

Now, we're going to bring both comps into a new comp, and will name it Sports Graphic main. We need to create a transition element to move in-between our two scenes. Let's re-use one of our flashing lights from the first comp. Simply copy and paste that precomp into the Sports Graphic main comp.

Let's use our lens flare to create a dynamic transition between our comps by following these steps:

1. Trim your Sports Graphic comp right where you ended that comp.

2. Place your Camera track comp underneath the Sports Graphic comp.

3. Move the Camera track shot to the left by one frame. Your comps should overlap slightly.

4. Delete all key frames from the light comp.

5. Position the light comp on top of both comps.

6. Move the light comp in the timeline between both layers, as indicated in the following screenshot.

7. Animate just the scale of your light from 0 to 5000, and then back to 0.

8. Your last key frame needs to be after the second comp begins, as indicated in the following screenshot.

Animating the light in this way will serve as a flash between both scenes. This should hide where one comp ends and the next one begins. The following screenshot demonstrates what the final graphic will look like:

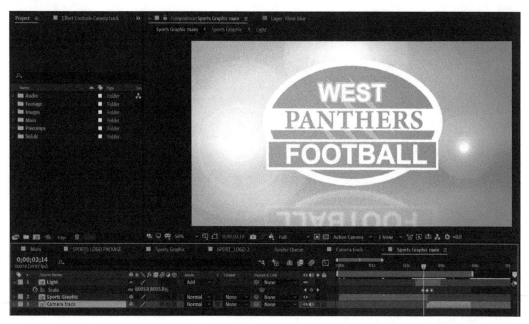

The transition

Unique transition effects are important in creating your projects. These can be simple but visually impressive, and can be used in interesting ways in different video projects.

Summary

Congratulations! You have created an awesome sports graphic project! We have learned how to create a dynamic composited video project. Understanding how to track video footage, apply color correction, and apply lighting effects will help you to create convincing, professional quality projects. The tools are used in movies, television, and music videos. Anytime you see a 3D element in a movie, it is using 3D tracking software. Traditionally this process is done using an expensive camera tracker. But now, After Effects has its own camera tracker, and you know how to use it! Now, you can track a shot and add 3D elements to it all in After Effects. How cool is that! Movie standard effects at your fingertips! This chapter sets the tone for our next lesson on combining visual effects, live action footage, and 3D camera tracking. Join us in the next chapter, where we will continue working with effects, and learn about camera tracking.

Questions

1. What's the name of the effect we used for our light effect?
2. What's the name of the color correction effect used in this project?
3. What is it called when a video scene move creatively from one scene to the next?
4. What is the blending mode we used to composite our light into our scene?
5. What's the effect used to track footage?
6. After tracking footage, what are the colorful x marks on the footage?
7. What are the red discs we look for after tracking?
8. How do you make a layer 3D?

7

Developing a VFX Project Using the 3D Camera Tracker

In this chapter, we will learn how to use the powerful compositing tools that After Effects is known for. Compositing is the process of bringing all of your VFX elements together in a convincing way. Compositing is a skill that is used in virtually every visual effects shot in the movie industry. This will be increasingly important as you continue working with motion graphics. In this chapter, we will focus on taking a scenic shot and replacing elements in the shot with photos. We will cover the following topics:

- Creating a polished shot-replacement video
- Using the 3D camera tracker
- Using the Quick Selection tool
- Using color-correction effects
- Compositing photos into tracked footage

Creating a VFX shot

In this section, we will focus on getting up to speed creating visual effects for your shots. This will help you take another step toward developing Hollywood feature-film quality in your work. The 3D camera tracker in After Effects is one of the most powerful features that the software has. It allows you to add new objects in the 3D space that match the movement and perspective of your footage. You can composite something into a scene that was never there.

Analyze footage

Imagine you're a visual effects artist working on a film. The director asks you to record footage and add a new red car to the scene to help to tell the story. The goal of this VFX shot is to seamlessly add a photographic element to existing footage.

Let's add a red car into the scene. The first thing we need to do is import our footage and analyze it, taking a look at the footage and its attributes, including the frame rate. Our footage is 1,920 x 1,080 with a 29.97 fps frame rate. We want to match all of these settings exactly. An easy way to do this is to drag our footage down to the New Composition button and then go through the following steps:

1. Create a new project.

2. Create folders for Footage, Main, Precomp, and Images.

3. Drag the footage into the **New Composition** tab. This will create a new composition with matching frame rates and so on for the footage.

4. Critically look at what's going on in the footage.

Take a look at the following footage attributes:

Footage attributes

This footage was shot with a camera on a tripod. You're working with high-quality footage. It should be clear and at least 1,920 x 1,080. Not all footage tracks well in the camera tracker. In fact, poorly shot footage will fail in the tracker. It works best with smooth footage, without the camera moving around a lot. It works best if there aren't too many objects moving in the scene. You will have the most success with panning down, panning left to right, pushing in, pulling out, aerial shots, and walking or driving scenes. Once we've confirmed the quality of the footage, we're ready to use the camera tracker.

How to use the 3D camera tracker

The 3D camera tracker works by analyzing the footage in your comp. It looks for high-contrast areas and tracks those areas in the scene. It tracks the 3D data, recreates the scene that was shot with the camera, and adds a 3D camera in the scene. Let's set up our footage to track it. We are going to edit the best shot in this footage.

Let's trim our footage to the best scene in this clip; the camera tracker will track only the trimmed footage. Trimming your footage will reduce your track time. To trim your footage, go through the following steps:

1. Go to 2:18 on the timeline. Trim the beginning of your footage at this point on the timeline.

2. Go to 7:05 on the timeline. Trim the end of your footage at this point on the timeline.

3. Move your footage to the beginning of the timeline, as shown in the following screenshot:

Trim footage

The **3D Camera Tracker** analyzes your video and lets you create an After Effects camera that matches how the original sequence was shot. It creates track points, solves the track points, and creates an After Effects camera for the scene.

To track your footage, add the **3D Camera Tracker** from the **Effects & Presets** menu:

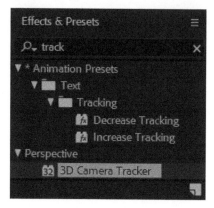

3D Camera Tracker effect

Adding this **Camera Tracker** effect to your video layer will create a 3D tracked scene. Go through the following steps to create your camera track:

1. Add **3D Camera Tracker** to your footage from the **Effects & Presets** menu
2. Wait while your footage is analyzed

After your track is complete, you will see a variety of track points in your scene, as shown in the following screenshot. These track points are data that your tracker has created based on the data from your video:

Track points

You're doing a great job with our track project so far. If you can't see your track points, go through the following steps to ensure that they can be viewed:

1. Select the footage in the timeline

2. Select the effect in the effect control panel

3. Make sure that the **Show Layer** control is on

Please ensure that the effect is selected and that **Show Layer** is on to see all of your track points, as shown in the following screenshot:

Show Layer Controls

At this point, we need to think about what our goal is with the shot. We want to place a car in the parking lot. We need to find track points that will be at the correct angle for our image. Drag your mouse over the scene in which you will see the targets appearing. These target points are positioned at different angles and sizes, as shown in the following screenshot. We are looking for a target that faces the camera directly. This will match the car we are going to add to the scene. These targets need to line up so that they have the correct perspective:

Target

The next step is to choose the type of object we will attach to our track points. Go through the following steps to create a solid:

1. Right-click on your target. You can add text, a solid, or a null.

2. Choose a solid, as demonstrated in the following screenshot. When you select this option, the target will be replaced with a solid layer and a camera will appear in your timeline:

Create Solid

You're doing a wonderful job! We have done a lot in this project so far. We've applied the **3D Camera Tracker**, analyzed the scene, solved the camera, created a 3D camera tracker layer, and tracked points. Now we're ready to attach a photo to the camera tracker points.

Selecting and cutting out images

Now that we have successfully created a tracked solid to our scene, we need to add a car to our scene. Take special care when selecting your elements so that they properly fit the perspective of the scene. We are going to add photos to our video scene, with the goal of fooling the eye and making our photos look like they belong in the scene.

When choosing images, remember that objects should appear smaller as their distance from the viewer increases. Also, the angle of the object should be in alignment with other objects in the scene. Look closely at the video for any grain or special lighting or shadows in the scene. Keep all of these things in mind when selecting your images. Our scene is a simple left-to-right camera pan, so I am going to choose a car that fits that perspective.

Now that you're aware of how to choose your images, go through the following the steps to put the car on a transparent background:

1. Open the image of the red car in Photoshop.
2. Choose the magnifying glass icon on the far left.

3.   Click on the image to zoom into it. Let's use the **Zoom** tool to get really close to our image, as shown in the following screenshot:

Zoom tool

Now that you know how to zoom into your image, let's use the **Quick Selection** tool to select our image.

Quick Selection tool

One of the most important things you need to know in motion graphics is how to cut things out. You need to know how to cut your subjects out of an image and place them on a new background. It has never been easier to make selections and cut things out in Photoshop. The following steps will show you how to do this:

1.   In the far left of the interface, choose the **Selection** tool.
2.   Click and drag on the outside of the car.

3. By default, the selection tool has a + sign next to it, which means it will add to your selection as you drag the brush.

4. Press the *Alt* key to subtract from your selection. There is a simple pop-out description when you hover your mouse over this tool for more information. The following screenshot displays the instructions for the **Quick Selection** tool:

Quick Selection

Drag inside the car image until it is completely enveloped by the dashed lines.

In doing this, the **Selection** tool recognizes the contrast between the red car and the background. Adjust your selection until you're happy with it. When your image looks similar to the following one, we can proceed with creating a vector mask for it:

Car selection

Now we are going to create a vector mask for our selection. This is a nondestructive way to cut our car out of an image, but we can always go back and edit it, even after bringing it into After Effects. Go through the following steps to create a vector mask:

1. Navigate to the far right of the panel.

2. Look at the lower left-hand side. Choose the vector mask symbol:

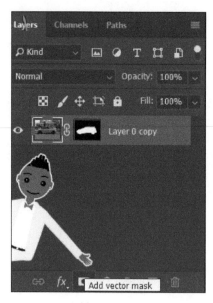

Add vector mask

Clicking on this tool will immediately create a cutout for you. This checkerboard pattern means your car is on a transparent background. The great thing about this form of masking is that it's nondestructive and continuously editable. You can use the paint brush to add or subtract from this mask. You can also feather your edges to soften your mask. Create a selection like the following car:

Vector masked car

Now that we have cut our car out, we can bring it into After Effects and place it in our scene.

Compositing our scene in After Effects

Let's jump back inside After Effects and import the car we just cut out. We are going to composite it into our scene. When you import the car, choose to import it as a composition and retain the layer size, as shown in the following screenshot.

This will ensure that you have your layer on a transparent background and that it will come in the size of the layer, not the canvas size:

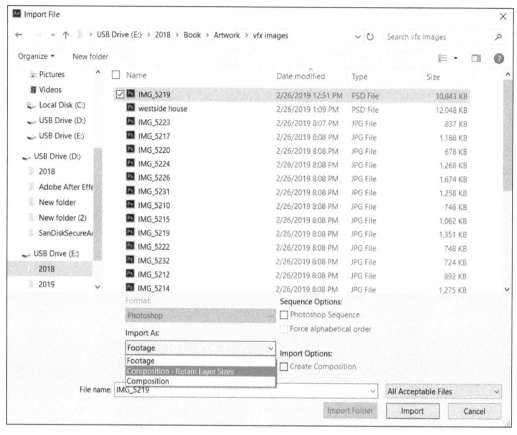

Import composition

Your file will come into After Effects as a composition. Let's incorporate the image into the timeline by going through the following steps:

1. Select your solid in your project

2. Find the car image in the project window

3. Drag the car into your timeline while holding down the *Alt* key

This is a handy shortcut that will replace anything as long as the Alt key is held down. Your solid should not be replaced by the car at this moment. Press the spacebar to preview your scene. You should see an image similar to the following screenshot:

Replace solid

Now that we have our car in your scene, we need to add some color correction to further composite the image into our project. Color correction can be used to fix irregularities in your images, and it can help fool the eye and make it look like the image belongs in the scene. This video has a lot of blue in it, so let's adjust the blue in the car using curves. Curves work by adjusting points throughout an image's tonal range. Go through the following steps to adjust the curves for this image:

1. Select the car.
2. Add the **Curves** effect.
3. In the **Effects** panel, choose the **Blue** channel.

4. Move the blue curve up slightly, as shown in the following screenshot:

Color correction with curves

Great job! You have effectively tracked a video shot, prepared an image for your scene, and composited your scene! I'd like to encourage you to think of other elements to add to your scene. Take some photos of trees or anything else you think might make your scene compelling. Now that you know how to track footage and create shot replacements, you can explore this further and bring what's in your imagination into reality.

Summary

In films, VFX is most successful when you don't notice it. In this chapter, we learned how to create VFX shots that look real. These types of shot can be used in movies, commercials, and music videos or to fix a shot. You have learned many skills and tools. You can take photos and edit them in Photoshop with the Quick Selection tool and cut the background out in a nondestructive way. You can also use the 3D Camera Tool to track your footage, and create a scene with all of your VFX elements composited realistically together. The biggest thing we learned was how to replace our solid with any image of our choice and composite our footage into a scene. You now have incredible tools to create believable visual effects that can be used in movies, commercials, and personal projects. Have fun experimenting with these VFX tools!

Questions

1. What is the name of the effect that is used to track footage?
2. What type of footage is best used for camera tracking?
3. What effect did we use to correct the color in our project?
4. What is the tool that we used to cut out an image in Photoshop?
5. What kind of mask did we apply to our image in Photoshop?

Section 3: Working with 2.5D, 3D

In this section, you will learn how to create a 2.5D animation. You will also learn how to use Cinema 4D lite to build and animate complete 3D scenes.

The following chapters are included in this section:

- *Chapter 8, Create a 2.5D Environment Camera Fly Through*
- *Chapter 9, Build a 3D c4d Lite Logo Project*

8
Creating a 2.5D Environment Camera Fly-Through

In this chapter, we will learn how to use the 3D tools in After Effects. We will continue building on the concepts we've only touched on in the previous chapters by creating a camera fly-through in a 3D environment! The 3D tools in After Effects are not true 3D tools—they are actually 2.5D. Using these tools gives us access to other dimensions, so we can move things along the Z-axis. This may sound simple, but it actually unlocks the ability to use a true camera and lights that interact with the layers in the composition. This means that we won't have access to full 3D capabilities unless we use a 3D program, which we will go into in the next chapter. For this project, we will use all of the assets from Illustrator. Artwork from Illustrator is vector-based and can be scaled without losing quality. This will be important as we zoom in close and fly through our scene.

The following topics will be covered in this chapter:

- 3D camera
- 3D lights
- Using different views
- Animating the 3D camera
- Using the graph editor

2.5D camera fly-through

3D cameras and 3D layers can be used to create graphics that are dynamic and lifelike. Understanding these tools will help you to create graphics that can be used in television documentaries or any media where you need to bring photos or illustrations to life. For this project, we are going to create a camera fly-through in three different environments. The important thing is that you know how to control your camera and set up your layers in 3D space. After Effects doesn't have true 3D space; instead, we utilize something called 2.5D. With this, you get the real Z-axis depth in your scene, but no rotational depth. We will limit our camera moves to the Z-axis for this project.

3D layers

In motion graphics, it's important to understand how to use 2D layers as well as 3D layers, and how to animate 3D cameras and 3D lights. The versatility of 3D animated layers and parallax camera movements are used in the creation of film titles, videos, commercials, and animated GIFs, along with documentaries and television shows. It's also crucial to know how to control your layers in 3D space so that they are spaced correctly in the 3D environment. Take some time to look at films with interesting camera movements and lights. How do the camera movements and lighting communicate information to the viewer? What makes these lights and camera moves interesting? How can you incorporate these techniques into your work as a motion graphic designer?

Any After Effects layer can be placed in 3D space. As soon as you enable the 3D layer switch, the layer becomes 3D. Let's create a blue and green layer and enable the 3D switch. The 3D switch is the cube icon shown in the following screenshot:

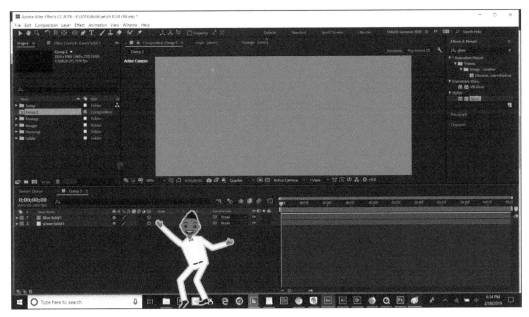

3D solid layers

Now that we have created our 3D layers, we are ready to add a camera to our scene. To really see our 3D layers, we need to see our scene from different views. We need to activate the **Select View** layout to see these views: front, left, top, back, right, or bottom. These views are useful for placing and previewing elements in a 3D scene. 3D layers appear in working 3D views; 2D layers do not appear in working 3D views. The next thing we are going to do is turn on the two-view option by going through the following steps:

1. Look on the lower-right side of your comp panel.

2. Look next to the **Active Camera** tab; click on the arrow next to the **1 View**. Take a look at the following screenshot. This is where your views are located:

Views

As you can see, you have different options for your 3D views. We are using the **2 Views - Horizontal**. Let's take a look at how our layers look in these different views. Select your layers and you will see that they have 3D handles, as shown in the following screenshot:

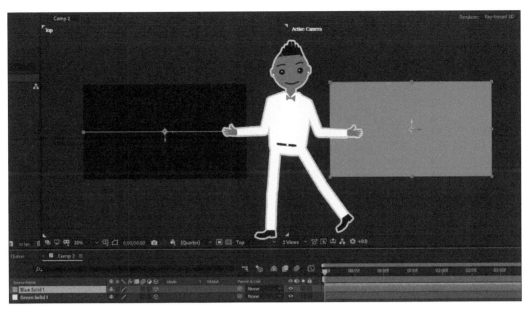

3D layers

The two views we are looking at here are the top view and the active camera. Whatever panel you click on will show the **Viewer** tab. You will also see blue triangles in the panel corners. This means that the view is active. When you make a layer 3D, the layer itself remains flat, but it garners additional properties such as **Position** (z), **Anchor Point** (z), **Scale** (z), **Orientation**, **X Rotation**, **Y Rotation**, **Z Rotation**, and **Material Options**. These position properties are represented by arrows. Grab one of these arrows and move your layer in 3D space.

3D camera

I hope you enjoyed moving layers in 3D space and looking at the scene in multiple views. However, the real fun begins when you add a 3D camera to the scene. 3D cameras allow us to move around in our scene and animate our view through the camera's perspective. To add a camera to your project, go through the following steps:

1. Select **Layer**
2. Click on **New | Camera...**

Create a new camera in the menu, as shown in the following screenshot. After you've added the new camera, you will see it appear in the composition:

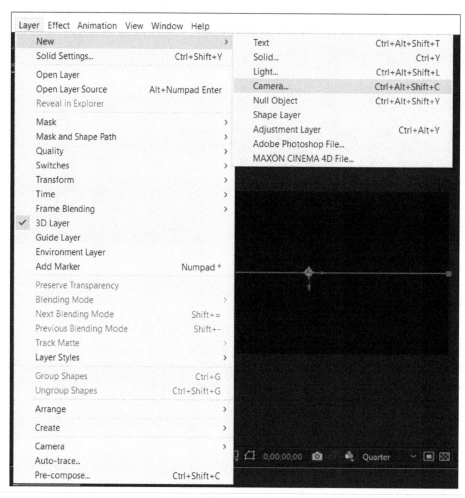

3D camera 1

Take a look at the following screenshot. These are the camera parameters. Your settings should look like the following:

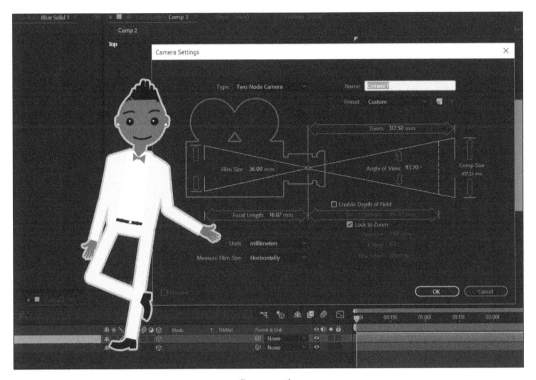

Camera setting

Now that we have our camera in our scene, you can see that the camera has 3D handles, just like the 3D layers.

Also ensure that your comp is set to classic 3D, which can be found at the top-right corner of your comp window. This is illustrated in the following screenshot:

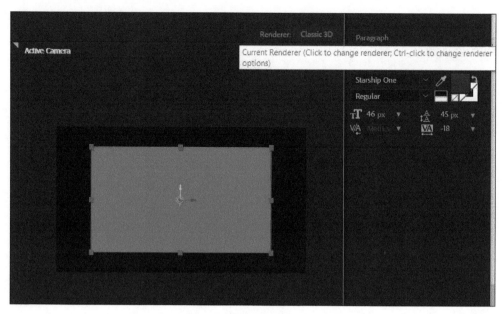

Classic 3D

Now, we are going to move our layers in 3D space. Select the bottom layer and move it back in the 3D space. You can do this by choosing the blue arrow and pushing your arrow back in 3D space, as shown in the following screenshot:

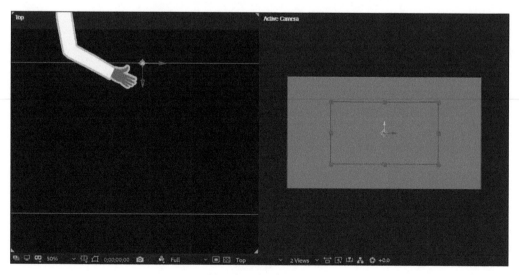

Move layer in 3D space

This will move your layer back in the space. You will see the layer moving in the active camera to the right.

Another way you can move your layer in 3D space is to scrub the far-right position parameter (the third row of numbers to the right). This is shown in the following screenshot:

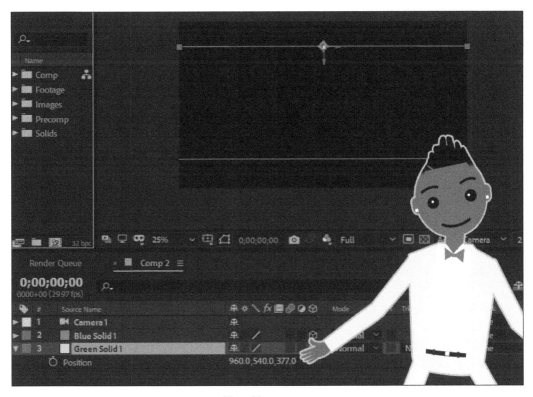

3D position parameter

You're doing a great job! You now know how to move your layers around in 3D space. Let's repeat the preceding steps and add multiple layers to our scene.

We are going to animate a camera pushing through three different environments. Let's look at our scene through multiple views. In our **View** tab, change the views to **4 views**.

This will show us all of the different views. Let's start by adding three solid layers for the environments. Go through the following steps to add more layers and position them correctly in our scene:

1. Duplicate one of our current 3D solids.

1. Evenly space the layers in 3D space. Look at the following screenshot as a reference for positioning your three solids in 3D space:

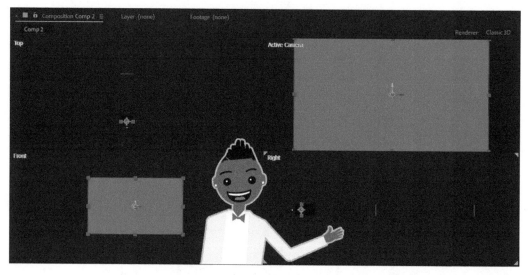

Positioning 3D solids

Note that the lower-right comp panel shows the right view; the square represents the camera and the red line represents the layers in 3D space. They have quite a bit of distance between them. Remember that you can move your layers by using the 3D arrows or the position parameters. It's easier when you're beginning to learn 3D to use the position parameter. This ensures that your moves will be more accurate.

Now that you have a significant distance between your layers, let's add more 2D solids to fill our environments out. To do this, we will add more layers in between our different layers. Look at the following screenshot and note the lower-right view. I have added 14 solid layers in my project. These are all spaced evenly. Space your layers accordingly. Remember to select the right view. If you don't, you won't see your layers active, as shown in the following screenshot:

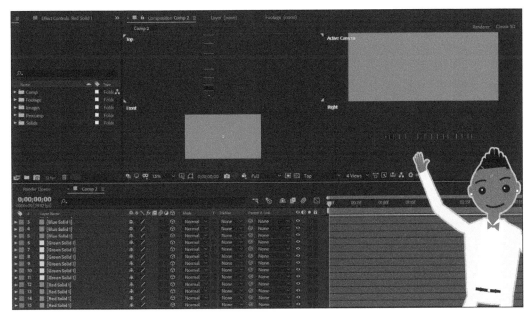

Adding 2D solids

Now we're going to start moving our camera in our scene. Let's first turn **Auto-Orient...** off on our camera. To do this, simply go through the following steps:

1. Go to **Layer**
2. Click on **Transform | Auto-Orient...** and switch **Auto-Orient...** to **Off**

By default, After Effects will try to orient your camera automatically. Turning **Auto-Orient...** off puts the power of controlling your camera in your hands. The following screenshot shows how to find and disable the **Auto-Orient...** function:

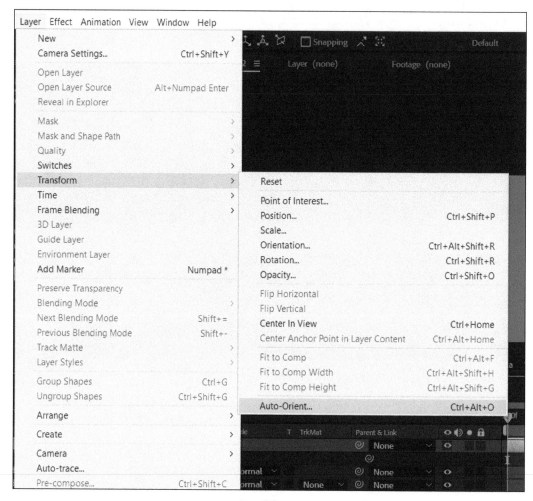

Auto-Orient...

Now we are ready to start moving our camera in our scene. We first need to add a 2D layer in our scene for the background. Go through the following steps to get started:

1. Move the current layer to the bottom of your layers.

2. Now, let's start moving our camera in the scene, change our view to the 1 view active camera.

3. To control your camera, use the **Camera** tools, located in the upper-left corner of the **Tool** panel, and choose the **Track Z Camera Tool**, as shown in the following screenshot. You can cycle through these tools by pressing the C key:

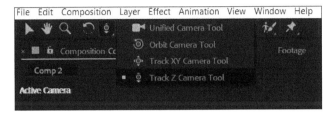

Camera tools

Using your mouse to click and drag in your scene will cause you to zoom in and out of your scene.

4. Pull your camera back in the scene so you have greater distance between the first layer and the camera.

5. Click and drag while holding down the C key until you have the **Orbit** tool.

6. Orient your camera so you're looking down on your layers, as shown in the following screenshot:

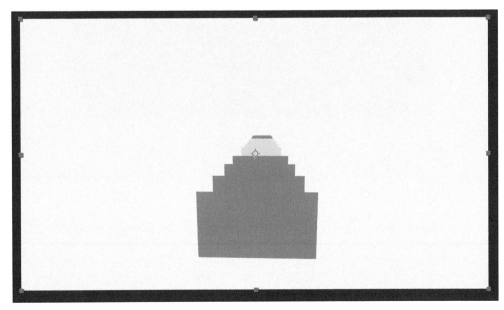

Camera orientation

Congratulations! You have your layers positioned in 3D space. Next, we are going to add lights to our scene!

Lights

Lights can really add a dynamic feel to your project. Just understand that turning on the shadows can also add more to your render time. Be selective when using shadows for your project. Now that you know how to move your camera around, let's bring some lights into your scene. Go through the following steps to get started:

1. Go up to the top of your interface and choose a new light layer. You can choose any light you want, of whatever color and intensity you wish. Play around with these settings. I am choosing a white spotlight.

2. Adjust your light positions. Move them back and to the left and right.

3. In order for your layer to cast a shadow, we have to turn **Cast Shadows** on. Choose the first layer in your composition. Under the **Transform** properties, you have something called **Materials**. Click on the **Materials Options** for the layer. Change this to **Cast Shadows**, as shown in the following screenshot:

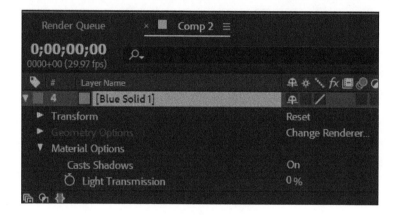

Cast Shadows on

Now that you have **Cast Shadows** turned **On**, your first image should cast a shadow, as shown in the following screenshot:

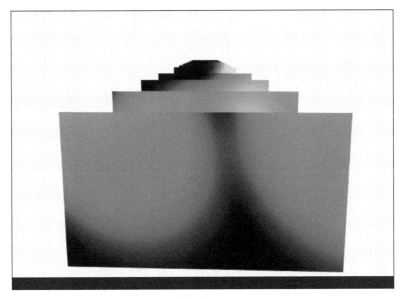

Shadows

For now, let's turn **Off Cast Shadows**.

You've successfully added 3D layers and lights to your comp and moved your camera around in your scene. Let's import our city scene into our environment by going through the following steps:

1. Import the `city` file from this chapter's assets folder

2. Choose to import it as a composition

3. Choose to retain the layer size

Great! Now you have your city art work in your project. It should come into the project with a folder of art work. We are going to just use the city buildings to start off; we will use the bridge in the project later.

Creating 3D environments

We are going to build an art scene in 3D space by using the city building art work. We will replace the solid layers in our comp with the city artwork. To replace the solid layer in the comp, go through the following steps:

1. Select the first layer in your composition

2. Go to the project window

3. Press and hold the *Alt* key (*option* on Mac)

4. Drag the city layer into the composition and let go of the *Alt* key to replace the solid layer

5. Turn on **Continuously Rasterize** for all of your layers to keep them sharp

This is how you will replace all of your solids in this comp and have them stacked in 3D space. You may want to practice this a couple times. The solid layer should be replaced with a row of city buildings. Use the hue saturation effect to change your layer to the desired color. Click the **Colorize** option after that to adjust the hue and lightness. Take a look at the settings I used to change the color of my buildings, as shown in the following screenshot. Adjust your buildings' color so that it looks right to you:

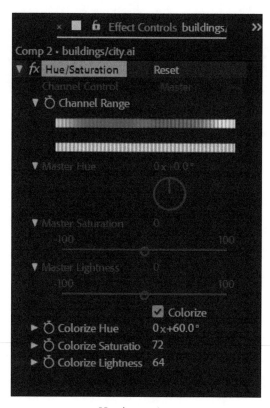

Hue/saturation

Scale up your building if necessary, then duplicate and move the position to the right. You should now have one whole row of city buildings. Go through the following steps:

1. Choose one of your first rows of buildings and duplicate it.

2. Leave it selected and choose the bridge layer from the project panel.

3. Replace the building layer with the bridge layer.

4. Adjust the color, scale this layer up, and position it in the scene. Ensure that you have turned on the **Continuously Rasterized** option for the bridge.

5. Duplicate the bridge and push it back a few rows in 3D space.

6. Repeat these steps for the next three rows stretching back.

I have changed the background of my scene to a blue and adjusted the colors, scale, and position of my buildings in 3D space. Look at the following screenshot to see how to set up your city environment:

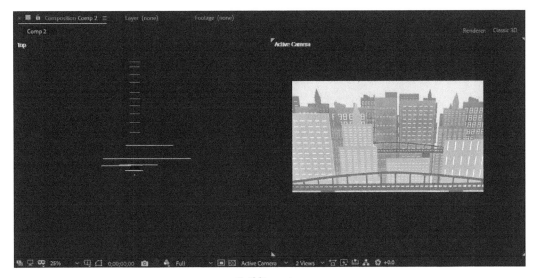

Building setup

Notice how densely packed the city environment is? Look at your view through the two views side-by-side to see how you've populated the first third of the environment in 3D space. The goal is not to see the bottom of the buildings or the bridges, so adjust your artwork's scale and position. Take your time creating this first environment because we are going to use the same steps to create the other environments. We want to animate the camera moving through a city scene, so we are going to create a couple more environments so that the viewer feels like they are going on a journey.

When you have finished with this environment, go through the preceding steps to create the environments for the trees. Use the trees to populate the environment as demonstrated in the preceding steps. After this, you should have environments for a city, trees, and a herd of deer positioned in 3D space, as shown in the following screenshot. Make sure your layers have enough distance between them so your camera can move dynamically through the scene. Did you note how I left a path between the buildings for the camera to fly through? Adjust your layers so the camera doesn't run into anything:

Spacing layers

Did you note how the layers are evenly spaced in the environment? They have quite a bit of distance between them, and there is an open path to fly the camera through.

Animating the camera

You're doing a great job! So far, we have learned about 3D layers and how to adjust and create a camera and lights. We've also learned how to replace layers with artwork. Now, we are going to animate a camera through our scene by going through the following steps:

1. Select your camera and set a key frame
2. Move down to the very end of your timeline
3. Move the position of your camera so it ends up in the last environment of the herd of deer

Your camera should be going through three different environments. You may need to adjust your layers if the camera is colliding with your layers. Our goal is to have only two key frames. If you need to adjust any of your key frames, do so at the beginning or at the end of the composition, where you already have key frames. Take a look at the following screenshot. Note how the camera has two key frames in the timeline:

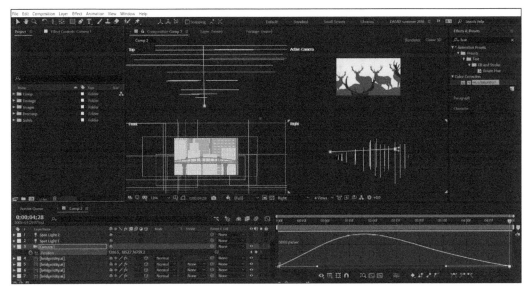

Camera animation

As you can see, your camera has a direct path to the last environment. Next, we need to ease the camera's movement. In the following section, we will use the graph editor to create a custom ease effect.

Using the graph editor

Let's ease our key frames with the key frame assistant. We can further edit the movement of our key frames by selecting the graph editor. To use the graph editor, go through the following steps:

1. Ease your key frames.
2. Select your key frames.
3. Look in the middle of the timeline above the lock icon. Click on the graph editor icon.
4. Click on the graph type.
5. Choose the **Edit Speed Graph**.

Now that you have switched on the graph editor (it's indicated by the highlighted blue graph icon in the following screenshot), you need to turn on the **Edit Speed Graph**. The following screenshot demonstrates where this is:

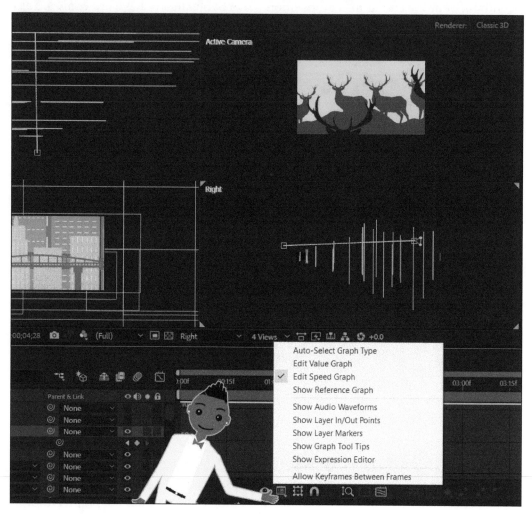

Graph editor options

This will allow us to edit the speed of our camera. Dragging the handles of the graph editor and creating more of a curve eases and slows down the movement of the key frame. Drag the right handle as shown in the following screenshot to make the camera ease into the last key frame. Make sure your key frames are selected before entering the graph editor options or you will not see the graph. When you are done with this editor, simply click the graph editor icon to exit this mode:

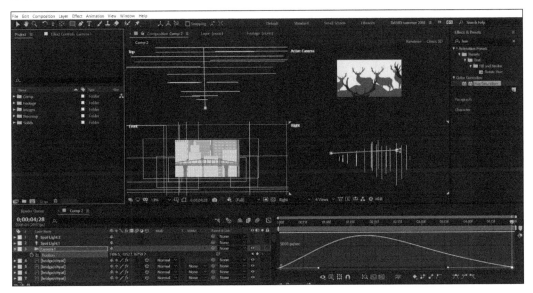

Graph editor mode

The overall effect we are going for with this project is to create a dynamic and smooth animated camera moving through a 3D environment. If you need to, adjust your camera movement and use the graph editor to create a pleasing camera movement. You can also adjust your layers and position them so they are evenly dispersed throughout the 3D space.

Summary

I am so proud of your hard work! You have created an awesome 3D camera fly-through! We learned how to create 3D layers and lights and animate a camera in a project. Understanding how to create 3D projects with cameras and lights will help you to create dynamic and exciting professional projects. You can use these tools in many different types of motion graphics jobs. These tools are used in movies, television, and music videos. Anytime you see a camera move in a video, consider how the camera moves. Remember, After Effects has 3D lights and cameras, and now you know how to use them!

This sets the tone for our next chapter, which deals with C4D lite. We will build and animate a logo in C4D lite. This program comes bundled with After Effects; it's a great way to build on what we've learned about 3D in After Effects and take that knowledge into a real 3D program to create a dynamic project. See you in the next chapter!

Questions

1. How do you create a 3D camera?
2. How do you add 3D lights?
3. What are the advantages of using different views?
4. How do you adjust lights?
5. Why should you use shadows with caution?
6. What key do you need to press when replacing layers with artwork?
7. Why should you turn on continuous rasterization?
8. What is the advantage of turning **Auto-Orient...** off?
9. What tool should you use to move the 3D camera?
10. What are 3D parameter handles?

9
Building a 3D C4D Lite Logo Project

Give yourself a pat on the back for making it to the **Cinema 4D (C4D)** Lite chapter; you're going to love it! After Effects and C4D Lite give you professional-grade tools at your fingertips that let you add 3D elements to your compositions. C4D Lite and After Effects together is a powerful combination! Just like with any of the Adobe software, these two programs work well together. The workflow is seamless; you can easily jump back and forth between the programs.

The following topics will be covered in this chapter:

- Creating a C4D layer in After Effects
- C4D interface
- Modeling a ribbon with sweep nurbs
- Importing Illustrator files into C4D
- Creating text in C4D
- Creating an eye with sweep nurbs
- Modeling a logo star
- Creating a camera in C4D
- Rendering C4D project from After Effects

C4D Lite 3D logo project

Getting started in the world of 3D is a blast with C4D Lite! 3D elements are used virtually everywhere in the entertainment world, including in sports graphics, television news graphics, and VFX-heavy movies. 3D projects are dynamic and exciting; they add another layer of realism to a scene.

Although C4D Lite is shipped with After Effects, it isn't the full version of C4D. This is just a basic lite version. Nevertheless, it's a great way to get started with C4D. We will learn how to model, light, and animate a logo. We are going to create an impressive 3D logo and add it to a project in After Effects. We will add the final touches to our project with compositing tools and render it out of After Effects. Let's begin!

Creating a C4D layer in After Effects

C4D is dependent on After Effects in a couple of ways. You need to open the program through After Effects. You have to render your project through After Effects and, once you've created a C4D layer, it can only be moved or edited through C4D. Never move or scale the C4D layer up in After Effects. To create a C4D layer, follow the steps:

1. Go to the **Layer** tab

2. Select **MAXON CINEMA 4D File...**

Refer to the following screenshot to create your C4D file in After Effects:

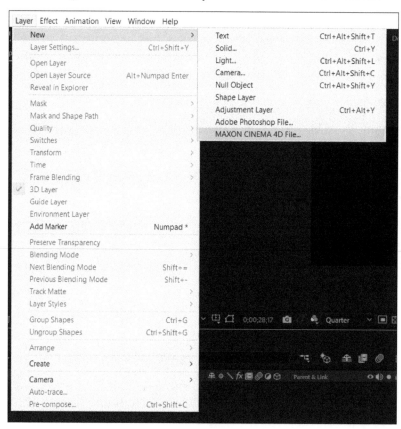

New C4D layer

Awesome! You've created your first C4D layer. In order to edit it, you need to save your project in After Effects. This will automatically save your project and create a C4D project for you. Follow the steps to open the 3D file in C4D:

1. Save your project.
2. Go to the **Edit** tab.
3. Choose **Edit** original. This will open the file in C4D.
4. Close the C4D information panel.

C4D interface

Let's take a tour of the tool panel in C4D; it's located in the same place as the After Effects tool panel. C4D's tools are intuitive and easy to understand, thereby allowing beginners to jump in and take control. Take a look at the tool panel in the following screenshot. You can hover over the tabs to see a full description of the tools and to familiarize yourself with their functions. If the tool has a triangle in the lower corner, it implies that clicking on it will reveal additional options:

Toolbar

The numbered sections represent the following:

1. Undo
2. Live selection tool
3. Move tool
4. Scale tool
5. Rotation tool
6. Last tool used
7. Render view
8. Render submenu
9. Edit render
10. Objects
11. Splines

12. Generators

13. Modeling submenu

14. Bend deformers

15. Add floor object

16. Cameras

17. Lights

The tools I want to draw your attention to are the move tools on the far-left side of the panel. These are important tools as you will use them a lot. We will cover these tools and more later in this chapter. You don't have to memorize all of these tools; just make yourself familiar with where they are located.

Let's start creating 3D objects right away! The basic shapes that ship with C4D are called **primitives**. These are the basic building blocks for modeling anything. The following screenshot show the different primitives available. Click on the **Cube** icon to add a cube to your scene:

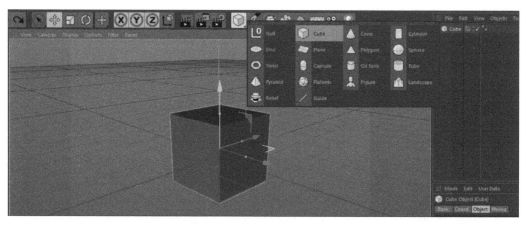

Objects

When you click on the Cube icon, the cube automatically appears in your project. To move or scale any object in your scene, use the move tools in the upper-right corner. You have access to the move tool, which allows you to move your object on the xyz axis. The scale tools allow you to increase the size of your object, and the rotation tool allows you to rotate your object. Just like in After Effects, these objects rotate around the axis point. Let's rotate our cube by clicking on the rotation tool. Rotate your object as demonstrated in the following screenshot:

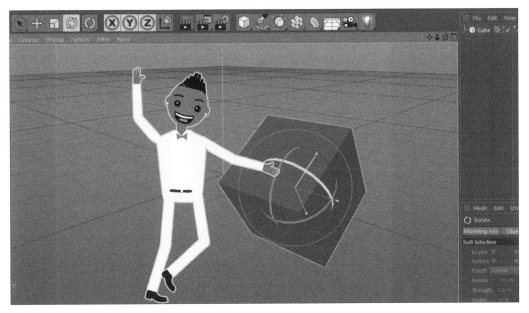

Rotate tool

Notice the colored bars; these represent the different parameters you can rotate your object around. Let's take a look at the navigation tools. Jump all of the way over to the upper-right corner of the project screen. These four little buttons enable you to navigate around your scene and to look at your project in different views. You are able to do the following:

- Move
- Zoom
- Rotate around in your project
- Look at different views

Click on the move tools to activate them. Take a look at the following screenshot to see where to find these tools in the upper-right corner of the panel:

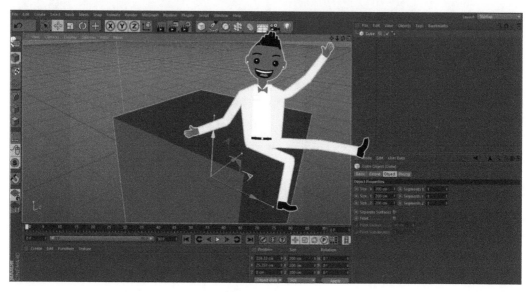

Navigation tools

You can further edit your cube by using the tools on the far-right of the screen. These modeling tools let you edit primitive shapes. Take a look at the following screenshot to find these tools:

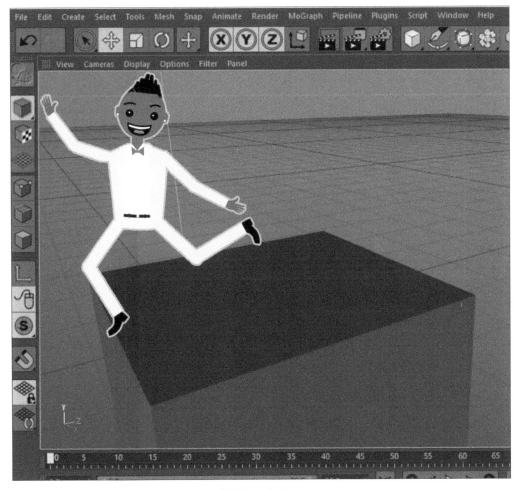

Editing primitives

We are going to make our cube editable so we can adjust the points. To make an object editable, do the following:

1. Select the object
2. Click on the Make Editable icon

Look at the following screenshot to help you to find the Make Editable button. One important note is that, once you've made your object editable, you can't reverse this function:

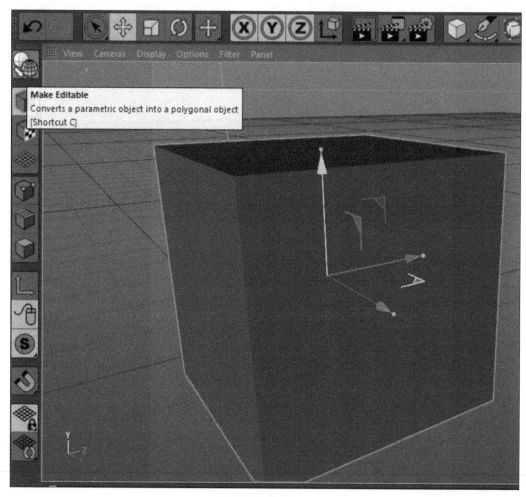

Make Editable

Now that your object is editable, you can further edit it. Let's adjust our axis point. The axis point is like the anchor point in After Effects. Your object moves around this point. To adjust the axis point, follow these steps:

1. Select the object
2. Choose the move tool
3. Click on the enable axis tab
4. Move the axis

Choose the move tool and pull the axis point as demonstrated in the following screenshot. Notice how the axis moves as you pull the handles. This is similar to using the Pan Behind tool in After Effects to move the anchor point of your layer:

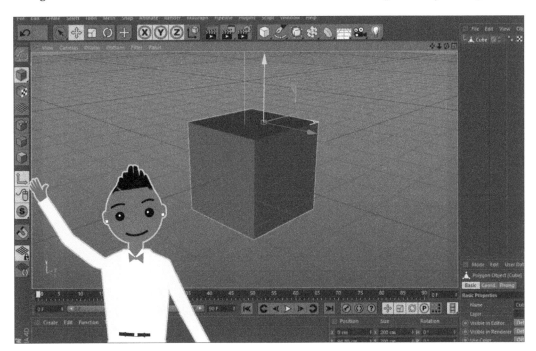

Move Axis

With our layer editable, let's enter the points mode to look at some of the modeling capabilities. Click on the point icon as demonstrated in the following screenshot:

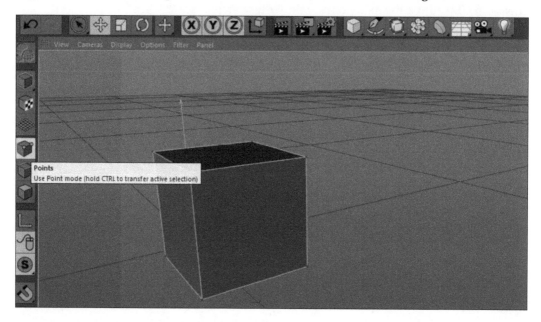

These points can be edited to begin modeling a new shape! To do this, click on the point and drag it, as in the following screenshot:

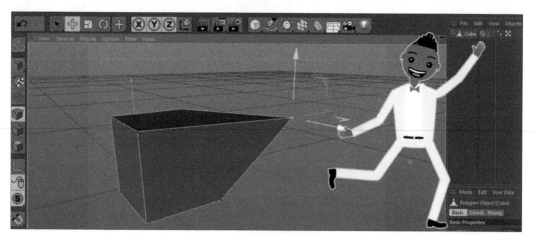

Drag points

The timeline in C4D is similar to the one in After Effects. In this area, you have the time indicator play button and the animation buttons. We will go over these in detail later in this chapter. Take a look in the following screenshot to see the timeline:

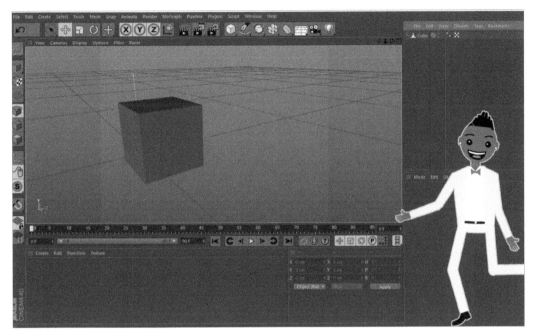

Timeline

You can edit your project settings by going to the **Edit** tab and selecting **Project Settings...**. The Project **Settings...** are indicated in the following screenshot. In the Project Settings..., you can customize the components of the project, such as turning on autosave:

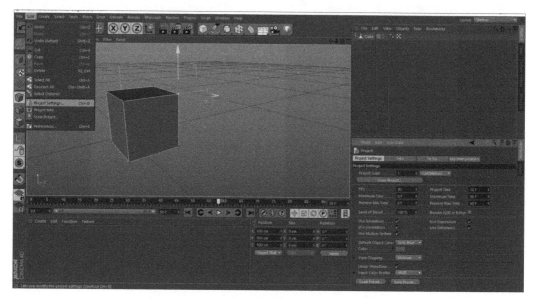

Project settings

Now that you have a basic understanding of the interface, we will begin creating our project for this chapter. We will go over more tools and panels as we progress. Let's start with modeling our first element for our logo.

Modeling a ribbon with sweep nurbs

We are creating a fun 3D logo that will be composited in After Effects and placed over video footage. In this section, we will begin modeling a ribbon for our logo. We are going to use the spline tool, which is just like the pen tool in After Effects. Enter the top view by clicking the far-right view port icon. Choose the top view in the upper-right corner. Look at the following screenshot to see where to find the view port icon:

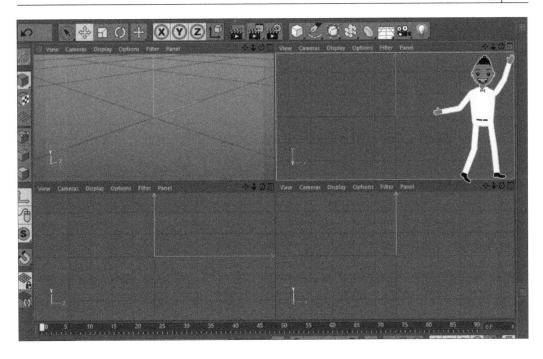

The top view port is ideal for creating a spline to model an object for our logo. Look at the following screenshot to see what the top view looks like:

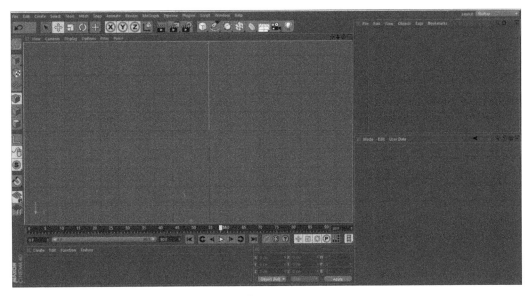

Top view

To use the spline tools, execute the following:

1. Click on the icon with the **Pen** on it. This will display all of the spline tools at your disposal.

2. Select the **Pen** tool.

Look at the following screenshot to help you to locate the spline tools:

Pen tool

Now we are going to create a banner ribbon shape by clicking and dragging the bezier handles. The following screenshot shows the creation of a path with the **Pen** tool:

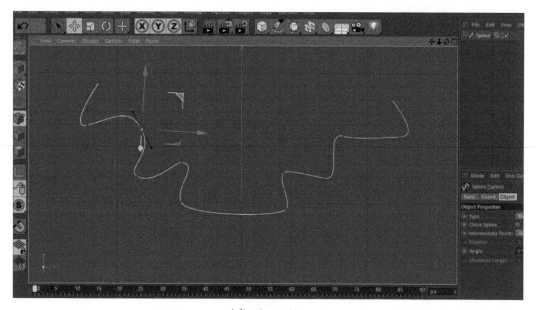

Adjusting points

Let's exit this view mode by clicking on the view port icon. Go back to the front view. As you can see, we have a spline that's parallel to the ground plane. Having your path parallel to the floor ensures the geometry of the ribbon will be correct; that why it's essential you model the path in the top view. Let's create some geometry for the spline to make it look more like a ribbon:

1. Click on the nurbs icon
2. Choose a **Sweep** nurb

The following screenshot is a reference for finding the **Sweep** nurbs:

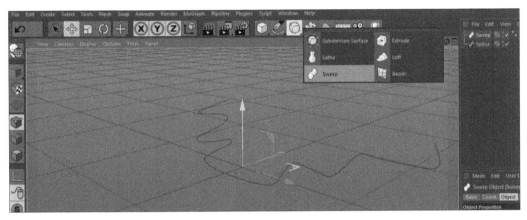

Sweep nurb

Next we need to add another spline to our object. Let's add a rectangle to help to model our object:

1. Click on the spline icon
2. Choose the rectangle shape
3. Choose the scale tool and scale down the rectangle
4. Place the rectangle and the spline object in the sweep object
5. Select the rectangle object
6. Increase the height of the rectangle so the ribbon's height increases

Look at the following screenshot to see what the hierarchy of your object must be like. Make sure you see a downward arrow as you place your objects in the **Sweep** nurbs object. The layers must look exactly like the following screenshot, in this exact order: **Sweep**, rectangle, and spline. These layers must be indented as indicated in the layer panel. This is how we will create many elements for our logo, so be sure you get used to this stacking order of your layers:

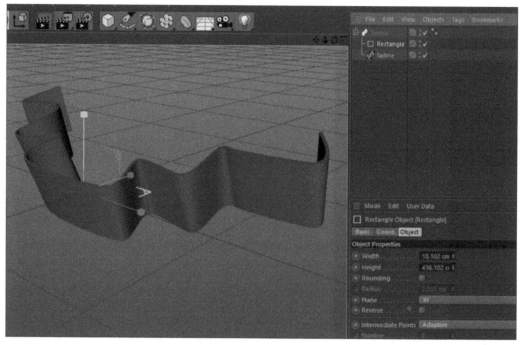

Ribbon

So far we have learned how to model an object with C4D; now let's explore it further by importing Illustrator files.

Importing Illustrator files into C4D

When you save your files from Illustrator, choose the Illustrator option. Here, you can choose the version you want to save your file as. Choose the old version of Illustrator 8; this version is compatible with C4D. See the following screenshot for the Illustrator **Version** option tab:

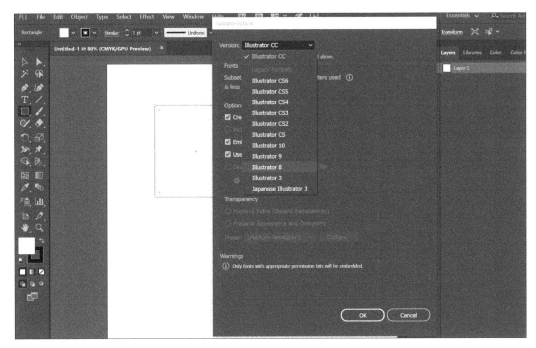

Illustrator version option

To import an Illustrator file, choose the **File** tab and click on **Merge....** This is the same as importing a file in After Effects. Choose your Illustrator file and merge it into C4D. See the following screenshot to find the merge function in the interface:

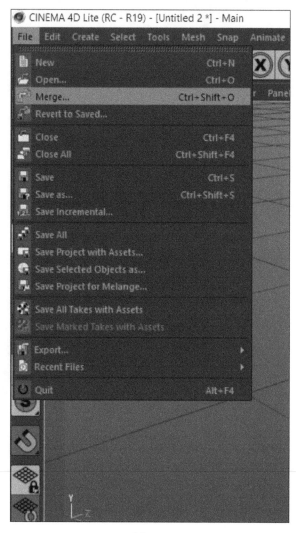

Merge

Now that we have our Illustrator file in C4D, let's have fun creating some geometry from it. Click on the nurb icon and add an extrude nurb to our project. This creates geometry for our path. As in the demonstration with the ribbon object, the hierarchy for the object is very important. Please follow the steps to extrude the Illustrator shape:

1. Put the path inside the sweep nurb object.

2. Select the object icon.

3. Choose a **Null** object.

4. Put the extrude object inside the **Null** object.

5. The Null object is similar to a folder; it allows you to group things together for organization purposes. Look at the following screenshot to aid you in creating a **Null** object:

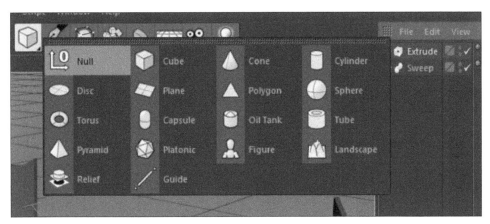

Null

Take a look at the following screenshot to see exactly how your objects should be organized. The Extrude object is inside the **Null**. This is also called making the object a child:

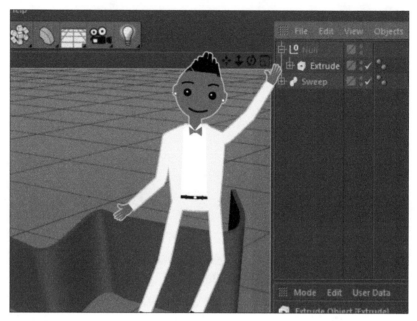

Null 2

Next, we need to edit the parameters for our object. Select the Extrude nurb and adjust the movement of the object. Adjust the far-right movement parameters to get the desired look.

Let's create the wings for our logo. We are going to follow the same steps as we did when we imported the crest shape. Follow these steps:

1. **Merge...** the Illustrator wings file into the project
2. Add the **Extrude** object to the project
3. Choose the **Extrude** nurb object
4. Check hierarchical
5. Adjust the far-right movement parameter as we did with the crest object

6. Create a **Null** object

7. Place elements inside the **Null**

8. Adjust the scale/position of the wings

Checking the hierarchical box will ensure that all of the paths will be extruded. Check this when you have a file that has multiple paths. Look at the following screenshot to see the hierarchical box to check. Also, notice the far-right movement parameter in the object properties panel; it has been adjusted to 20 to create the thickness for the wings object:

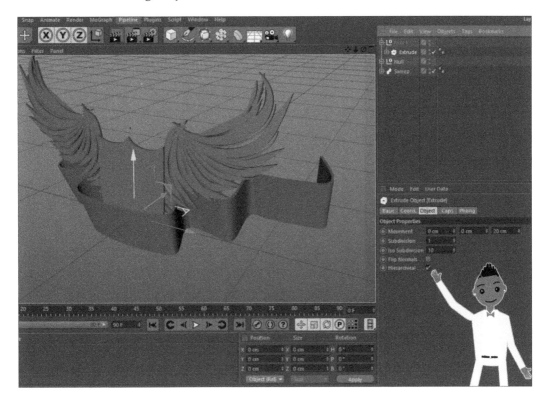

Hierarchical

Now that we have created elements for our logo, let's jump into the exciting world of 3D text.

Creating text in C4D

You're doing a great job with your C4D project! Let's create some 3D text with the text tool. The text tool is located in the spline tab. Navigate to the **Text** tool as indicated in the following screenshot:

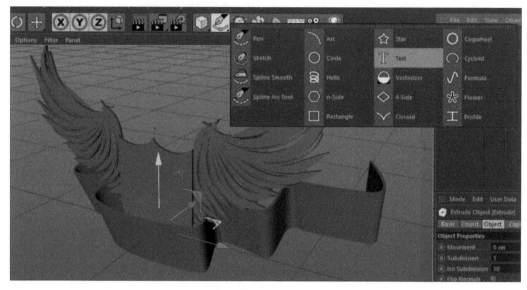

Text tool

To add a text object, follow these steps:

1. Click the spline tab
2. Click the **Text** tool

A text layer will appear in your project after selecting the Text tool:

Now let's type the word `imagine` in the **Text** tool object panel. This will create the text in your project. You can further edit your text's size, horizontal spacing, and the **kerning** of your text. In this panel, you also can select your fonts. Let's create geometry for our text by following the steps:

1. Use the **Arial Black** font for the text
2. Add an **Extrude** nurb
3. Make the text the child of the **Extrude** nurb

4. Create **Null** for the text objects

5. Name the text

6. Adjust the movement of the **Extrude** object (adjust the far-right movement parameter)

Refer to the following screenshot for the text-adjustment features:

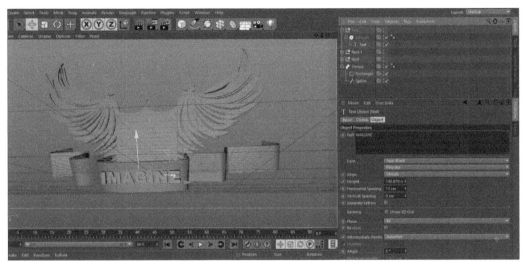

Text tools

Let's add some more detail to our text by adjusting the caps:

1. Choose text

2. Choose the **Caps** tab

3. For **Start**, choose **Fillet Cap**

4. For **End**, choose **Fillet**

5. For **Fillet** Type, choose **Engraved**

6. To extrude the caps, adjust the **Radius** amounts for the start and end parameters

Look at the following screenshot for reference. Pay close attention to the **Caps** parameters:

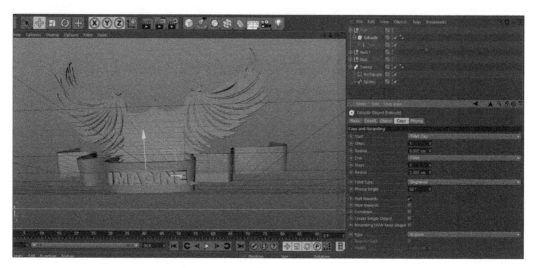

Caps

Your text should look like the preceding screenshot with a slight cap on the text. Next, we will create an eye element for our logo.

Creating an eye with sweep nurbs

We are going to create an eye shape for our logo. This process is similar to how we created the ribbon, however, we are going to create our basic spline from a ellipse spline object. You can find the ellipse spline in the spline menu. Follow the steps to create an eye shape for the logo:

1. Add a circle spline shape to the project
2. Adjust the scale of the eye so it fits in the center of the crest
3. Make the object editable
4. Choose the move tool
5. Adjust the side points to create an eye shape

When you are done with this, you should have an oval eye path. Next, we're going to create geometry for our path. We will follow the same steps we used earlier for the ribbon. Follow the steps to add geometry for our eye path:

1. Add a rectangle.
2. Scale down the rectangle.

3. Add a **Sweep** nurb.

4. In the layer panel, put the rectangle and the circle in the sweep object. The stacking order is sweep-rectangle-circle path.

You're doing a great job with your eye shape! Let's create a simple pupil shape to put inside our eye. We are going to use the same process we used for the crest shape. We will create a path then use the **Extrude** nurb to create the 3D geometry. Follow the steps to do that:

1. Create another circle path

2. Add an **Extrude** nurb object

3. Make the circle path a child of the **Extrude** nurb

4. Put all eye elements into **Null**

5. Name the **Null** eye

Look at the following screenshot to see the placement of the eye shape:

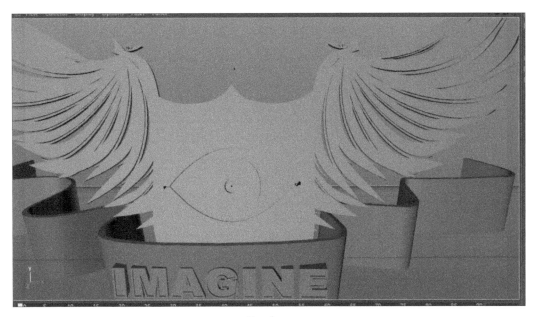

Eye shape

Now that we have our eye modeled, let's create a star shape for our logo!

Modeling a logo star

In this project, we are creating a detailed logo that will catch the viewer's eye. In order to build this logo shape, we will follow the same steps we used to create the eye oval shape, except we are going to use the star spline. Follow the steps:

1. Create ray elements from the star spline.
2. Make the star editable.
3. Add a rectangle.
4. Adjust the rectangle size.
5. Add a **Sweep** nurb.
6. Make the rectangle and star shape children of the **Sweep** nurb.
7. Put the rectangle above the star in the stacking order.
8. Put all elements in the null-label the null:

Star

Your star shape should look like the preceding screenshot. Next, we will start adding materials to our objects by using the material content browser.

C4D materials

Let's jump into the world of materials by going into the material **Content Browser....** This can be found in the **Window** tab as indicated in the following screenshot:

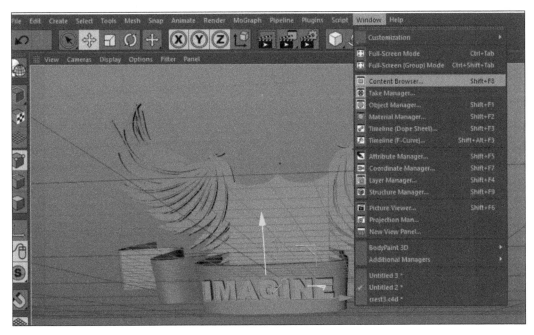

Material browser

After opening the content browser, you may be overwhelmed by all of the folders. C4D ships with tons of presets, lighting kits, and materials. Spend some time exploring all of these free goodies! (Click the arrows to go forward and back in the browser.) Let's explore the material presets. Follow the steps to add **Toony** materials to the logo:

1. Go to the `Presets` folder.
2. Click on the `Lite` folder.
3. Click on the `Materials` folder.
4. Choose the `Toony` material to add to our project.
5. Double-click the **Soft Green**, **White**, and **Pink** materials. This will add those to the scene.

See the following screenshot to find the soft toon colors in the materials folder:

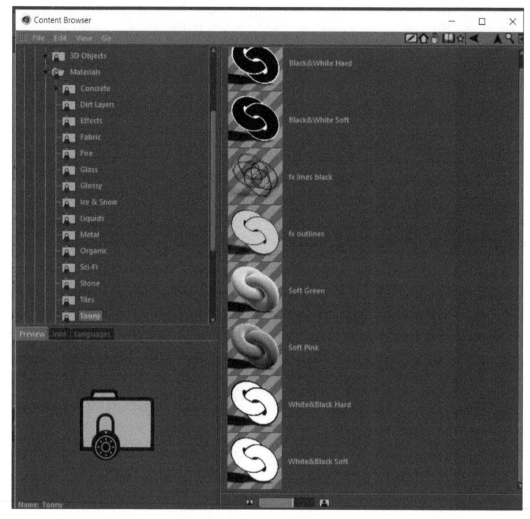

Toony materials

When you add the colors to your project, you will see them in the materials bin underneath the timeline. You can further edit these materials. Double-click on a material to edit the color. Let's change our colors to orange, light blue, and dark blue. If you want to add additional materials from an existing material style, follow these steps:

1. Select the material

2. Choose the **Edit** tab (directly above the material)

3. Choose **Copy | Paste**

This will add a duplicate of your material in the materials bin.

To add materials to your objects, simply select the material from the materials bin and drag it onto the object in the main composition. You will see an icon of that color in the layer panel. Additionally, you can add color to the caps for your text as well. Follow the steps to add color to your text caps:

1. Drag the colors you want to use onto your **Text Extrude** object.

2. Choose the material icon in the **Layer** panel.

3. Select the tag.

4. Choose the **Selection** in the tag panel.

5. Type C1 for the front color.

6. Type R1 for the side color. The following screenshot shows how to add multiple materials to an object. Look to the multiple materials on the far right of the object panel:

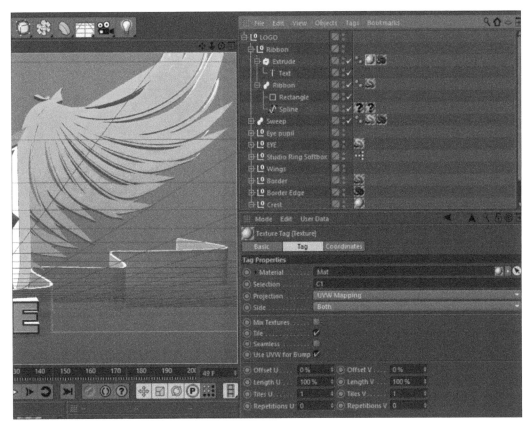

C1 materials

Adding materials this way, you can add multiple colors to your Text Extrude object.

Now that we have our materials for our logo, spend time adding color to all of the logo parts as indicated in the following screenshot. Choose the render view icon to see how your image will look when it's rendered. To activate this, simply click the render view icon.

You may want to hide things in your project. To hide things in your project, follow the steps:

1. Select the layer
2. Click on the red button in the layer panel

Notice I've turned off the border indicated by the red button. This will ensure this object will be hidden. To hide it and keep it from being rendered, follow the preceding steps but select the both button for the layer. See the following screenshot to locate the hide from view buttons:

Materials and labels

Now we have materials for our logo, let's jump into lighting in C4D.

C4D lighting

C4D ships with lots of professional lighting kits. Lighting is extremely important in 3D projects. Your scene comes alive when it's lit correctly. Choose a lighting kit that's appropriate for the type of scene you're creating. Let's navigate to the content browser and to the `Presets` folder. You can use the back arrow in the top-right corner to navigate the folders. In the `Presets` folder, there is a `Light Setups` folder. Choose the **Studio Ring Softbox** studio. This is selected in the following screenshot:

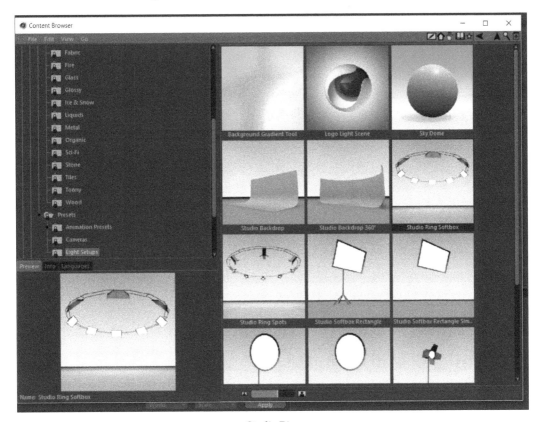

Studio Ring

Clicking on the lighting kit will automatically add it to your scene. We need to position it so it is in the correct position, as illustrated in the following screenshot. Move the lights so they are above the logo:

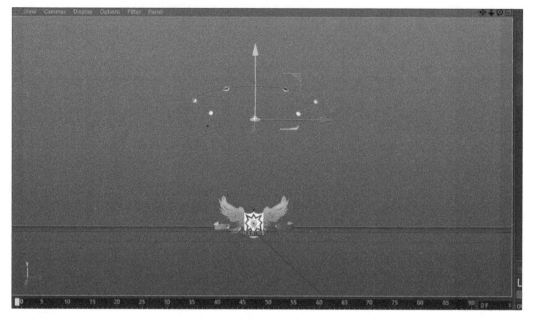

Light position

The lights in this scene are supposed to be soft light, so adjust them accordingly. Next, we are going to create a camera. We will not use this in our project, however, it's good to know where the camera is located.

Creating a camera in C4D

Adding a camera is done just like it is in After Effects. Simply click on the **Camera** icon. It will add it to your scene. However, you need to tell C4D to look through the new camera. To do that, follow these steps:

1. Add a camera to your scene
2. Choose **Cameras | Use camera**

Now, C4D will view your scene through the camera you created. The following screenshot shows you how to navigate the camera view options:

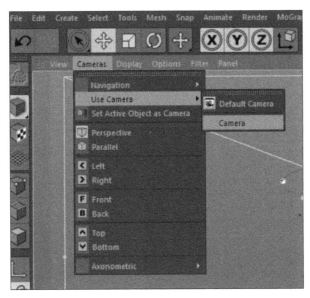

Camera

Let's delete the camera and start animating our logo. To animate anything in C4D, follow the steps:

1. Select the Record Active Objects button in the timeline. You will see a green tab in the timeline.
2. Move down in the timeline.
3. Change the position of the object.
4. Click on the Record Active Objects button.
5. You will see a new key frame in the timeline.

Look at the following screenshot to see how to activate the Record Active Objects button (the red key icon):

Record icon

Let's animate our logo. Put all of the logo layers into a null called `logo`. Now we can animate the logo in a group. We want the logo to spin around and resolve with it facing the front. Follow the steps to animate the logo:

1. Select the logo null.

2. Choose the rotation tool.

3. Click the Record Active Objects button in the timeline. You will see a green key frame timeline.

4. Move down in the timeline.

5. Rotate the logo so it rotates several times.

6. Click the Record Active Objects button.

7. You will see a new key frame in the timeline.

Follow these step for animating in C4D. By default, C4D eases your key frames to make your animations smooth:

Animation key frames

Now that we've animated our logo, we are ready to render it in After Effects. Before we jump into After Effects, let's adjust our render settings.

Rendering a C4D project from After Effects

In order to set up our C4D project for rendering in After Effects, we need to adjust our project settings first. Follow the steps:

1. Go to the Tool panel

2. Go to **Edit Render Settings**

3. Click on **Edit Render Settings** icon

This will give you the option to adjust the width and height of your project and the frame rate. Adjust your settings as shown in the following screenshot:

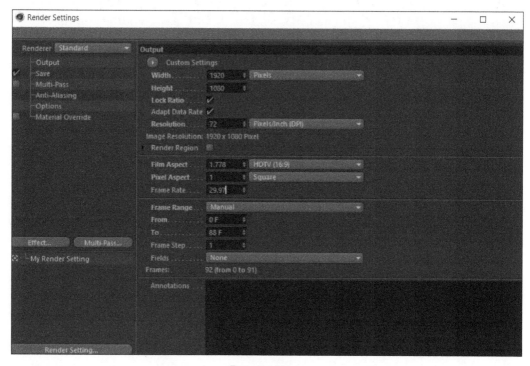

Project settings

Now that we have adjusted our settings, we can jump back into After Effects and continue editing our project. When you go back into After Effects, you will notice your C4D layer will be updated with a fully modeled scene. It may look different because the default view is a draft view. You will see the C4D floor in this view. To turn this view off, you have to change the render view to final. See the following screenshot for more clarity:

Final view

Let's add a video to our background in After Effects. Spend some time color-correcting the video so it looks like the preceding screenshot. Make best use of the hue/saturation effect. One important note is that you cannot change the scale or position of your C4D layer. Ensure that you make changes in C4D and save it and jump back into After Effects. Add the additional changes in After Effects by following the steps:

1. Color-correct the logo
2. Color-correct the background
3. Add the motion blur effect to the adjustment layer
4. Add a cc vignette to the adjustment layer
5. Jump back into C4D to make changes
6. Turn on Standard Final before rendering

Summary

Congratulations! You've come a long way from the first introduction chapter to now creating and animating a logo in C4D Lite. You can use C4D Lite to create 3D logos for personal projects or for clients. You have learned many skills and tools to create and import Illustrator files, import them into C4D, and make them 3D. You can also add materials and light to your scene as demonstrated in this project. The biggest things we learned were how to bring our 3D project into After Effects, edit it with effects, and render it to produce high-quality 3D video. This will help you to add value to your video projects. It also adds to your diverse skillset. We learned many different ways to model objects in C4D Lite. Experiment with these modeling tools so that you can master this craft. This has been quite a fun journey and I hope you continue to practice all that we've learned and become a lifelong fan of After Effects.

Questions

1. How do you create a C4D layer in After Effects?

2. How do you save an Illustrator file to import into C4D?

3. To create 3D text in C4D, what nurb do we use to create geometry?

4. What do we click to create an initial key frame in the timeline?

5. What do you need to turn on in After Effects before rendering a C4D project?

6. Can we adjust the C4D layer in After Effects?

7. What do we click on to edit the render settings in the C4D project?

Assessment

Chapter 1: Getting Started with After Effects

1. Choose a parameter to animate, hit the stop watch for that parameter, and move in the time adjust that parameter.

2. Hover over the end of the layer, identify the trim icon, and drag the layer. Use the shortcut *Alt + [or]*.

3. Go to the desired location in the timeline and press *N* or *B*.

4. On the lower-left side of the main window, choose grid and guide options.

5. Go to preview panel and press the next frame key. Use the *Page Down* keyboard shortcut.

6. In the preview panel, press play. Press the spacebar.

7. **Layer | New solid.**

8. Top toolbar.

9. Select mask and click once on one mask point.

10. Select mask and double-click on one mask point.

11. Select mask, twirl mask features, and choose subtract.

12. It marks the beginning of your animation in the timeline.

13. Blue diamond shape in the timeline.

14. The s letter on the timeline.

Chapter 2: Creating a Lower Third for a Television Show

1. A pen tool is used to cut things out with mask. Clicking and adding points creates a custom mask.

2. Select the key frames and drag them in the timeline.

3. An assistance tool designed to control how your key frames begin and end.

4. A tool to smooth your key frame movements.

5. Click on the text icon.

6. Add a null layer and parent the desired object to the null object.

7. Select the desired layers and choose composition precompose.

Chapter 3: Using Shape Layers to Create an Animated Lyric Video

1. A style added to your layers

2. **Layer | Layer Styles**

3. Vector layers that have shape parameters and animation parameters

4. A creative way to take you to the next scene

5. *Shift* + number + click on a number to add a note

6. A visual representation of an audio layer

7. An effect added to text layers to create instant text animation

8. **Effects presets | Animation presets | Text**

Chapter 4: Creating an Infographic with Character Animation

1. Tracking is used for the spacing between text.

2. Import as composition, retain layer size, and create a composition.

3. So they will look crisp, no matter how much they are scaled up.

4. This will give your animation a realistic smooth movement.

5. Turn on the camera control and microphone input icon. Hit the record button to activate live recording.

6. Go to file and choose export PNG and WAV file.

7. Two.

Chapter 5: Producing a Film Title Project Using Text Animator

1. Using one image as a way to hide or reveal parts of another image

2. **Layer | New | Light...**

3. Adds dimensional highlights and shadows to your type layer

4. A way to control the hue, saturation, and brightness of an image

5. A lighting effect that simulates a lens flare

6. An effect that changes the black and white values of the layer it's applied to

7. A guide to place text and other layers without it getting cut off by the edges of the television screens

Chapter 6: Animating Sports Graphics with Compositing Effects

1. Lens flare

2. Auto levels

3. Transition

4. Add mode

5. Camera track

6. Track points

7. Target

8. Click on the 3D cube icon

Chapter 7: Developing a VFX Project Using the 3D Camera Tracker

1. 3D camera tracker
2. Smooth camera moves
3. Curves
4. Quick selection
5. Vector mask

Chapter 8: Creating a 2.5D Environment Camera Fly-Through

1. **Layer | New | Camera**
2. **Layer | New | Lights**
3. You can accurately position and animate 3D layers in different views
4. Move the position parameter or the 3D parameter handle
5. They add significantly to your render time
6. The *Alt* key (*option* for macOS)
7. So that your layers will render at high quality
8. You have total control of your camera and your layers
9. The camera tool
10. Way to control a 3D layer represented by arrows on a 3D layer

Chapter 9: Building a 3D c4d Lite Logo Project

1. **Layer | New | MAXON CINEMA 4D file**
2. Save as illustrator 8
3. **Extrude** nurbs
4. The red record active object button
5. Final render
6. No
7. Render editor

Other Book You May Enjoy

If you enjoyed this book, you may be interested in these other book by Packt:

Mastering Adobe Captivate 2019 - Fifth Edition
Dr. Pooja Jaisingh, Damien Bruyndonckx

ISBN: 978-1-78980-305-1

- Learn how to use the objects in Adobe Captivate to build professional eLearning content
- Enhance your projects by adding interactivity, animations, drag and drop interactions, and more
- Add multimedia elements, such as audio and video, to create engaging, state-of-the-art learning experiences
- Use themes to craft a unique visual experience that reinforces the learning process
- Use question slides to create SCORM-compliant quizzes that integrate seamlessly with your favourite LMS

- Make your content fit any device thanks to the responsive features of Adobe Captivate

- Create stunning immersive 360° experiences with the all new Virtual Reality projects of Adobe Captivate 2019

- Integrate Captivate with other applications (such as PowerPoint and Photoshop) to establish a professional eLearning production workflow

- Publish your project in a wide variety of formats including HTML5 and Flash

Leave a review - let other readers know what you think

Please share your thoughts on this book with others by leaving a review on the site that you bought it from. If you purchased the book from Amazon, please leave us an honest review on this book's Amazon page. This is vital so that other potential readers can see and use your unbiased opinion to make purchasing decisions, we can understand what our customers think about our products, and our authors can see your feedback on the title that they have worked with Packt to create. It will only take a few minutes of your time, but is valuable to other potential customers, our authors, and Packt. Thank you!

Index

CPSIA information can be obtained
at www.ICGtesting.com
Printed in the USA
LVHW070719100822
725607LV00007B/47

9 781789 345155